Nati

COUNSELLING and COPING

KERRY GIBSON

LESLIE SWARTZ

ROB SANDENBERGH

OXFORD
UNIVERSITY PRESS

OXFORD
UNIVERSITY PRESS

Great Clarendon Street, Oxford ox2 6DP

Oxford University Press is a department of the University of Oxford.
It furthers the University's objective of excellence in research, scholarship, and education by publishing worldwide in

Oxford New York

Auckland Bangkok Buenos Aires Cape Town Chennai
Dar es Salaam Delhi Hong Kong Istanbul Karachi Kolkata
Kuala Lumpur Madrid Melbourne Mexico City Mumbai Nairobi
São Paulo Shanghai Singapore Taipei Tokyo Toronto

and an associated company in Berlin

Oxford is a registered trade mark of Oxford University Press
in the UK and certain other countries

Published in South Africa
by Oxford University Press Southern Africa, Cape Town

Counselling and Coping

ISBN 0 19 571868 2

First published 2002

Commissioning editor: Arthur Attwell
Editor: Jacqueline Irwin
Indexer: Mary Lennox
Cover designer: Chris Davis
Designer: Chris Davis

Published by Oxford University Press Southern Africa
PO Box 12119, N1 City, 7463, Cape Town, Southern Africa

Set in 9.5pt on 13 pt Meta plus by RHT desktop publishing, Durbanville
Reproduction by RHT desktop publishing, Durbanville
Cover reproduction by The Image Bureau, Cape Town
Printed and bound by Clyson Printers, Maitland

Contents

Acknowledgements

For some years, all of us worked at the Child Guidance Clinic of the University of Cape Town. Though this book was written after we had all left the Clinic, the book owes a great deal to our shared experience there, and we are very grateful to all the colleagues and students with whom we worked. Without their support for the development of our model of community-based counselling, this book would probably never have been written. A special word of thanks needs to go to the supervisors who played a key role in developing our approach. We are grateful as well to the many individuals and organizations with whom the Clinic worked. As is always the case, we probably learned most of all from clients and community-based partners. Rädda Barnen (Swedish Save the Children) generously supported the Clinic for many years.

Arthur Attwell of Oxford University Press has been a tireless and supportive Commissioning Editor who worked miracles in getting three busy professionals to make deadlines and, more remarkably, to stick to them. We are very grateful as well for his substantive input into the design, style, and structure of the book.

In spite of the help we have received, we alone are responsible for this book, and for any of its shortcomings.

Introduction

It is not just psychologists, social workers, and counsellors who care for the emotional needs of others; many people are involved in this work, including nurses, teachers, police officers, emergency workers, clergymen, managers, and volunteer community workers. While some of these people may offer direct counselling services, in many cases important therapeutic work happens in less formal conversations between care-workers and their clients as well as their colleagues. An aim of this book is to challenge the conventional idea that counselling is something that only happens in a formal consulting room between a client and a trained counsellor. This book aims to help people working in a variety of ways within a wide range of organizational contexts to develop their capacity to respond sensitively to others' emotional needs.

Counselling and Coping offers a different approach to the many books that propose a set of techniques aimed at improving people's counselling skills. We have found, through much consultation and training work with those in the human services, that while learning specific techniques in counselling is valuable, these learnt skills depend on a good, solid understanding of human relationships. We have tried to show how the ability to be a good counsellor does not just involve learning a new set of behaviours, but rather draws deeply from our knowledge about ourselves, our own emotional responses, and the understanding we bring to our everyday relationships.

We have also tried to emphasize how important it is for counsellors to not only look after their clients but also to look after themselves. Burnout remains a very real threat to those in the human services. Finding ways to cope with the demanding nature of this work is essential. We believe that the most effective counsellors are those who understand and respect their own emotional needs as well as those of their clients.

Finally, we have tried to offer a broad overview of counselling in the human services while also highlighting particularly challenging areas of work. We know of course that there will be some differences in the way that these ideas can and should be implemented in different settings and hope that our readers will feel free to adapt these ideas creatively and flexibly to meet their particular needs.

Kerry Gibson, Leslie Swartz, and Rob Sandenbergh

CHAPTER 1

Knowing ourselves

Self-knowledge is an asset for those who work in the human services. Drawing from our own experiences can be an important source of knowledge about our clients. Sometimes, however, our own personal issues can get in the way of understanding others.

Julia's story

Julia had just taken up her first teaching post at a local high school. She loved teaching and found that one of the parts of her work she liked the most was chatting to her pupils informally after classes. She spoke to them about their lives, their interests outside of school, and also about their personal problems which they increasingly began to confide in her. Julia had always known that people could speak to her easily and she was often the person her friends would turn to for a sympathetic ear in times of difficulty. In many ways, her role with the students was a familiar and comfortable one for her.

In the short time she had been at the school, Julia had already gained a reputation among her colleagues for being able to understand the emotional needs of her pupils. With no full-time counsellor at the school, some of the other teachers had started to ask for her advice on how to deal with children who seemed to be experiencing problems. Some had even begun to try out Julia's suggestions for a more sensitive approach to working with their students. These teachers were surprised to find that a bit of understanding often went a lot further in producing good school results than some of the more authoritarian methods they had tried before.

Julia had not had any formal training in counselling. She had, however, been a shy and withdrawn teenager herself, and found that she drew extensively on her own experiences to help her think about how some of her pupils might be feeling. She believed that it was through her own difficult experiences that she had developed a keen understanding of the emotional ups and downs of adolescence. The pupils instinctively seemed to recognize the understanding she offered, and told her things that few other adults got to hear about. Julia felt that just by talking informally with some of her pupils she had been able to give them something she herself had longed for during her own lonely teenage years – someone who would listen and understand. She also found that her involvement with the students in this way gave her a very deep sense of satisfaction in her work, and helped her to feel that what she did really *could* make a difference to their lives.

The kind of role that Julia fulfils in this school is very similar to that of a counsellor – she listens to the pupils' problems and is recognized by both them and the school itself to be a valuable resource in thinking through these and related issues. Although some people who find themselves doing this kind of work may have a formal qualification in counselling, clinical psychology, or social work, there are also many like Julia who are simply drawn to this role through a natural affinity and a good capacity for human understanding. In all sorts of organizations – schools, hospitals, churches, NGOs, and even businesses – there are many people who have recognized that part of their work in the human services inevitably involves providing emotional care as well as other more practical support. In some cases, this care might be given in recognized counselling sessions. Perhaps more often though, it is provided through less formal, but no less helpful, 'conversations' where a person simply provides support by listening and understanding. In either case, these people – whom we can think of as care-workers – often play a vital role in helping their 'clients' get the emotional support and understanding they need to help them manage their lives more effectively.

Despite the demands involved in taking on the problems of others in this way, there are fortunately many people like Julia who are willing to provide emotional care for others, either in a full-time or volunteer capacity. Whether they are working as nurses, teachers, youth workers, trauma counsellors, or psychologists they seem to share a strong desire to help others; to ease their emotional or physical pain, or to comfort them in their distress.

For many of us who are involved in this kind of work, it seems to satisfy a deeply personal need in addition to our more logical career aspirations. Perhaps part of why this work 'matters' to us in this way is because it connects with our own experiences. There certainly seems to be some truth in the often-quoted idea of the 'wounded healer' – the person who is driven to help others because of her or his own experiences of pain or difficulty. It seems that these kinds of experiences are extremely important in motivating caregivers to enter the human services, and to remain there despite the considerable emotional and practical demands this kind of work makes of them.

This personal connection to the work we do is valuable in that it gives us our capacity to empathize with the feelings of our clients and better understand how they might be experiencing things. It is important, however, that we also recognize that this kind of personal investment can, like most personality characteristics, act as a source of both strength and weakness in any work we undertake. Our own painful experiences may be a profound and irreplaceable source of knowledge, compassion, and determination to help. But they may equally create areas of 'blindness', an overly-close identification with our clients' problems, or personal distress, all of which can get in the way of our capacity to be effective helpers.

We believe that a better understanding of our own personal motivations and areas of vulnerability will enable us to make the best possible use of our own knowledge and experience to help others. In this chapter we illustrate the way in which the capacity for *self-reflection* can help us to draw effectively on our own emotional experience in order to help others.

Let's have a look at how Julia uses self-reflection to help her understand her own emotional responses to a student's attempt to share a problem with her.

Making it better

One afternoon, Julia was marking books in her classroom when one of her pupils, a young girl named Kershni, approached her shyly and asked if she had time to talk to her about something that was worrying her. Although Kershni attended one of Julia's classes, they had never spoken to each other alone before. Julia had noticed over the past several weeks that Kershni seemed reserved in class, had few friends, and disappeared the moment the bell went for the end of school. She had been feeling slightly concerned about the young schoolgirl and had been hoping for an opportunity to talk with her in order to try and find out in some way whether she was really as lonely as she appeared to be. So Julia was pleased at this unexpected approach and invited Kershni to sit down.

Speaking hesitantly, Kershni said that she was struggling to keep up to date with her schoolwork and was beginning to worry that she might fail the year if she couldn't keep up. Julia knew that Kershni, a very capable student, was certainly in no danger of failing. But she also understood that the young girl was clearly worried and upset about *something*. Before she offered a quick reassurance about the quality of Kershni's work, Julia felt she needed to find out what was really going on.

"I can see that something has upset you – can you tell me about it?" Julia asked gently.

In response to this soft prompting, Kershni's eyes filled with tears and she began to speak. She explained that her mother had recently been diagnosed with cancer and was now in hospital. Kershni had to leave school early every day in order to catch the bus to visit her. By the time she got home it was late and she was too tired, and often too upset, to attend to her homework properly. Kershni explained that she was an only child and that her father worked long hours. It was up to her, she said, to see to her mother. "It's just that I don't want to get into trouble about my work," Kershni said.

Julia felt her throat constrict and tears prick at the back of her eyes as she thought of this fourteen-year-old child trying to manage a situation that most grown-ups would find immensely difficult. "Don't worry about the work. You're a good student and you will be able to catch that up," she said. "It's awful though about your mom...," Julia added, aware that this was what was really troubling the young girl.

"Yes," said Kershni, "she's very sick. They say at the hospital that there's no more treatment they can give her." Kershni began to cry openly.

Julia found herself feeling increasingly distressed for the young girl as she helplessly watched her crying. Somehow in that moment she felt herself wishing that she were able to offer her something more concrete than sympathy. Eventually she reached across to pat Kershni on the shoulder and without really thinking said,

"Try not to worry too much about it. Things will get better."

Kershni's face suddenly registered an anger that took Julia by surprise. "You don't understand," Kershni said accusingly. "It'll never get better. How can you say it will!" Kershni dried her eyes and quickly got up and left the room, leaving Julia feeling confused and upset.

It is clear that Julia's talent for talking to her pupils about their difficulties comes from a genuine desire to help and a strong emotional connection with their experiences. This is an extremely valuable capacity and is one of the basic building blocks for becoming an effective helper. It is, however, also clear that although Julia was initially able to provide enough of a feeling of safety and comfort to allow Kershni to talk, towards the end of their conversation something went wrong with her very well-intentioned attempt to help.

Couched in a request for help with schoolwork, Kershni almost certainly came to Julia with some hope of talking through her difficult situation. Although Kershni had begun to express some of her distress about her mother, the discussion ended abruptly when she seemed to become angry. For her part, Julia felt frustrated by her inability to help, and distressed that she seemed to have misjudged what was needed. Despite the strong sympathy she had felt for her distraught pupil, she ended the conversation with the clear knowledge that Kershni had not, in the end, felt comforted by her.

The sense of understanding between the pupil and her teacher was broken when Julia offered the unrealistic reassurance that things would get better, despite the fact that what Kershni was obviously struggling with was the probability of her mother's impending death. Clearly it would have been the most helpful to Kershni had Julia simply talked to her about how she was feeling, and listened with minimum interruption. This would have given Kershni the much-needed opportunity to express some of her feelings about the impossible situation she found herself in, and to begin the necessary process of coming to terms with the pain of losing her mother. Instead, because of Julia's remark, Kershni was left feeling misunderstood and alone with her distress. She more than likely also felt that her situation must really be unmanageable if even this caring and sympathetic adult had to pretend that her mother was going to get better.

Although Julia could not have known this at the time, her reaction was in fact quite similar to Kershni's father's response to the situation. Unable to deal with the terrible thought of losing his wife, he had been putting up a falsely cheerful front at home that made Kershni feel even more alone with her pain than ever. Julia's comment had only served to compound this feeling.

Self-reflection

It is probably obvious to most of us who do counselling in some form or another as part of our work, that a glib reassurance is not the most helpful response in this kind of situation. Counselling manuals tell us clearly that it is best to stay focused on what it is the person is feeling and to simply reflect this, rather than offer what will immediately be recognized as a false solution to a difficult or irresolvable problem. Yet despite our knowledge of these things, it is interesting how often even those of us with considerable experience in various kinds of formal and informal counselling find ourselves tempted to do just what Julia did. Think how often, for example, teachers assure pupils that with their help they *will* pass their exams, or social workers promise that a child will not get into trouble at home for speaking out about abuse. Clearly, most helpers are not in any position to deliver on these kinds of promises and making them can cause a great deal of harm and embarrassment in addition to the kind of understandable anger that Kershni felt.

It is tempting to want to treat this kind of situation as an error that should not be repeated. It is, however, far more helpful and realistic to accept that these kinds of 'mistakes' are an inevitable part of helping relationships, and to create a space in which we can think about what they mean and reflect on the clues they give us about our own strengths and weaknesses in our work. In fact, our greatest source of knowledge can come from thinking about ourselves and the kinds of feelings that make us say and do the things we do.

To continue with our example, it would certainly not be helpful to Julia, or even to Kershni, to make a judgement about what has occurred between them. In order to make sense of their situation, it would be far more useful to consider (as we have already briefly done) what it might mean for Kershni. It would also be very helpful, as we have said, to look at what Julia as the counsellor can learn from this predicament about herself, her work, and her involvement in this situation in the first place. We start with the question of *why* Julia responded in this particular way (as indeed any of us might have) and illustrate how careful reflection on her own motivations and responses can help to develop her skill in understanding.

Despite the fact that she was an inexperienced teacher, Julia had a fairly remarkable potential to engage sensitively and helpfully with people. She did not need to be told that the reassurance she had given Kershni had been misplaced. After the incident, she sat at her desk wondering how she had ended up saying something that she felt was so uncharacteristically rash and so unhelpful. She could not help feeling angry with herself, and feared that she may have lost her only opportunity to help Kershni with her difficulties. Later in the staffroom, she found herself discussing the situation with one of the more senior teachers – a woman who fortunately also had a gift for listening sympathetically. "I just couldn't seem to help myself," Julia explained. "I just wanted to say something that would make her feel better."

Her colleague listened kindly and encouraged her not to view how she had reacted as a failure but as an opportunity to learn something about herself that might be of use to her in her work. Taking this sensible advice, Julia spent some time that evening trying to make sense of what had happened. She carefully tried to piece together what she had been thinking and feeling while she spoke to Kershni. What she recalled was being overwhelmed by the girl's sadness and a sense that it was unfair that someone so young should have so much to deal with. As she thought, she began to see that Kershni's particular situation had somehow touched a chord inside her, reminding her of some of her own experiences at a similar age.

Although both of her parents had fortunately remained healthy, they had divorced when Julia was in her early teens. Living with her mother, Julia had felt the separation from her much-loved father intensely and had felt very much alone, burdened with her mother's unhappiness and loneliness. It seemed, Julia realized, that she had connected too closely with Kershni's distress at the potential loss of her parent. Although her situation was of course different, like Kershni she had had to carry too heavy a burden for a young girl, a burden that at the time had felt just as unmanageable as Kershni's. As she thought about her own situation, Julia realized how much distress she still felt about this lonely and difficult time in her life that she thought she had put behind her. Thinking about it, however, she recognized that this experience had, in part, also led her into her current work and to her special feeling of connection to her young pupils.

This insight into her own response not only allowed Julia to think about her 'mistake' more compassionately, but also reminded her of the considerable store of knowledge she had to draw on in understanding her pupils. Using this knowledge, she could well comprehend the disappointment Kershni must have felt in an adult who seemed unable to understand how burdened and afraid she felt. Julia imagined how, in similar circumstances, she too would have felt angry at being asked to pretend that things were okay when they clearly were not. Somehow, rather than making her feel worse about her mistake, all this thinking seemed to leave Julia feeling less defensive and more kindly both towards Kershni and herself.

The next day Julia waited until the break and then called Kershni aside. She told her that she had thought about their conversation of the previous day and had realized that Kershni must have felt angry and upset with her for saying that things were going to get better. "It must have seemed like I wasn't really listening to you properly when you told me that your mother was very ill and could die," said Julia rather bravely.

Kershni put her head down and nodded slightly. There was a short silence in which Julia worried that she might not be able to regain this young girl's tentative trust in her. Finally, Kershni lifted her head and asked, "Can I come and speak to you later? I want to know what I should say to my Mom if she asks me how I'm managing."

"Of course," said Julia, feeling greatly relieved. Perhaps she would be allowed an opportunity after all to give Kershni the kind of help that she herself would have benefited so much from as a child.

Common difficulties in care work

Julia's situation is, of course, not unique. Many of us are driven into different forms of caregiving precisely because of the ways in which they resonate with our own experiences. It is not uncommon for someone to feel motivated to become a teacher, for instance, because of a difficult struggle to learn at the hands of an unhelpful teacher or school system. Equally, many nurses are attracted to the nursing profession because of particular experiences of illness – their own or those of a close relative. In all these cases, as with Julia's, it is the difficulty or pain of their own experiences that allows the people involved to be touched by the needs of those they work with.

Julia comes close to crying as she listens to Kershni talk about her situation. This shows that she has heard and registered her distress – an important starting point for any helping relationship. But instead of using her sympathetic response to deepen her understanding of Kershni's unique experience, Julia instead becomes overwhelmed by her own feelings and memories. Facing the double burden of her own emotional pain and that of her pupil, she is unable to think clearly about what would really be helpful in this situation. She finds herself compelled to try and make Kershni feel 'better', in much the same way perhaps that she hoped to have got over her own emotional distress around these kinds of issues.

Julia was fortunate to have been able to talk about her experience with a colleague who in turn encouraged her to reflect on the situation, rather than simply treat it as a 'mistake' deserving of punishment or apology. In this way, Julia was given the very important opportunity to consider her experience in a manner that was thoughtful, open, and above all, not overly self-critical. Many of us may find ourselves needing this kind of encouragement from our colleagues in order to get past a tendency to judge ourselves too harshly and allow us to freely explore our motivations and their implications for our work. As many of us know, however, it is not always easy to find someone to talk to in the middle of a busy day. It is therefore important to try and build up a capacity for self-reflection that can help us think through our own particular responses to our work and in this way, deepen our understanding of ourselves and of others.

It is quite likely that another person may have had an entirely different response to the emotional pain described by Kershni. The important thing is for each of us to identify our own particular motivations and areas of vulnerability that may influence our responses to our work. What makes us want to help people? What distresses or hurts or angers us when we do? It is important to reflect on the effects that these answers may have on different clients, and also on what we can learn about ourselves from them. If we think about our own reactions, some of us might find that we have a tendency to respond in a relatively constant way to our clients' difficulties, or we might find that we shift our pattern of response depending on the client we are working with and the feelings they evoke in us. Knowing more about ourselves will give us the tools to remove the obstacles to understanding that all of us carry in different ways and to establish true empathy with our clients.

What is empathy?

The following story describes the difference between apathy, empathy, and sympathy.

A man who had fallen to the bottom of a deep well was shouting loudly for someone to come and help him. A passer-by heard his cries but continued on his way. His lack of compassion left him *apathetic*. Another man who passed by a little later heard the same cries for help. He felt overwhelmed with distress about the man's plight and driven by *sympathy*, threw himself into the well where both he and the original victim remained helplessly stuck. A third man passed the well and heard the cries of the two trapped men. With *empathetic* understanding for their distress, he called out that help was on its way and quickly fetched a rope ladder which he let down to enable them to escape.

Empathy then is the ability to understand another person's distress, without either ignoring its significance or being overwhelmed by one's own emotional response.

Source: This story is adapted from one told by Renos Papadopoulos of the Centre for Psychoanalytic Studies, University of Essex.

Although our individual responses to listening to and understanding emotional pain will always depend to some extent on our unique histories and life experiences, there are some feelings that seem to be common to many of those involved in offering emotional care to clients. These typical reactions partly seem to occur because everyone finds it difficult to hear about and witness emotional pain. Partly though, as we have shown, the valuable emotional connection that many care-workers feel to their work may also make them particularly vulnerable to certain sorts of reaction.

Julia's response to Kershni's problems is a good example of a common difficulty caregivers might experience. In this situation, Julia is drawn out of her usual empathetic response towards a less helpful kind of sympathy by her own close identification with Kershni's difficulties. Recognizing elements of her own painful memories in the story that Kershni is telling her, Julia starts to confuse the client's experience with her own. It is this confusion that leaves Julia feeling overwhelmed – as if what Kershni is saying has actually happened to her. Julia begins to imagine that their experiences must be identical.

This *over-identification* leaves her flooded with her own unmanageable feelings and unable to deal with Kershni's. In another situation, this predicament might even lead care-workers to offer inappropriate advice based on their own experiences – as if their clients require an identical solution to their problems. The difficulty with this is that while we can learn a great deal from things that we have gone through, no single person's experiences are *exactly* the same as anyone else's. If we begin to believe that they are, this can prevent us from seeing the uniqueness of our client's experience. Ideally we should be able to recognize the points of connection between our experiences – to enable us to empathically imagine something of what our clients are feeling even when they don't describe this openly – but remain aware of the limits of our knowledge.

Julia's response also demonstrates another common reaction care-workers often have to the distressing experiences of others. Confronted with the very painful feelings people sometimes bring to us, many of us may feel that we ought to be able to offer something that goes beyond simple human kindness. The worse the pain described, and the more strongly we feel it (for whatever reasons in our own history make us particularly susceptible), the more we seem to feel that we should be able to magically do something to 'make it better'. The idea that we need to be *all powerful* may lead us, like Julia, to offer more than we can realistically deliver. As we have seen, however, this creates problems for both caregiver and client.

In our example, Kershni knows quite well that Julia is providing a reassurance that is blatantly false given her mother's terminal illness. As a result, she is left with the confirmation that her present situation must indeed be unmanageable if it cannot even be acknowledged by the adult she turns to for help. Julia, on the other hand, feels her own helplessness even more strongly. If she measures herself against the impossible task of 'making it all better' she can only come away from the situation feeling that she has failed. It would be more realistic if she allowed herself to recognize that Kershni's situation is inevitably going to be terribly painful for her. Facing up to this reality, Julia could then aim to try and support Kershni as much as possible by being there for her to talk to and offering a shoulder for her to cry on whenever she needed it.

Partly because of this kind of powerful desire to help, many of us may find ourselves getting *over-involved* with our clients' difficulties.

Marco was working as a youth worker at his local church and really enjoyed his contact with the teenagers who came to the youth club. It was partly because of his own troubled teen years that, like Julia, he felt a strong affinity with their view of the world. For the most part, this shared perspective made him very popular with the children, but it eventually resulted in some difficulty.

Ben, a sixteen-year-old boy attending the youth group, had made a particular impression on Marco. With his rebellious attitude towards any authority and the tough exterior he presented to the world, Ben reminded Marco of himself at the same age. He knew that Ben's father was a harsh and rigid disciplinarian who seemed overly critical of his son. Marco suspected that Ben used bravado, like he himself used to, to cover up his real feelings of insecurity and hurt. When Ben informed Marco that he had stopped attending school and was spending his time meeting with friends at the local shopping area, Marco became very worried about him. This particular area was known to be a common meeting place for drug dealers and was the site of frequent clashes between gangs.

Marco felt that he couldn't risk losing Ben's trust by talking to his parents about the situation. Instead, he decided to offer his own house as a meeting place for Ben and his friends. Marco's home soon became the key meeting place for a number of young boys who increasingly began to abuse his hospitality by smoking and drinking and even, he suspected, using drugs – all of which Marco had expressly forbidden. Marco felt trapped in the situation he had created and didn't know how to prevent his home from being used in this way by the boys.

When a group of parents finally discovered where their children were going each day, they were understandably very angry with Marco and blamed him for leading them astray. Marco felt ashamed of his involvement (however well intentioned it had been) but also rather relieved to have found a way out of the difficult situation.

In this example, we can again see that it is this care-worker's valuable sense of connection to the boys with whom he works that also represents his area of vulnerability. Marco understands from his own experience how hard adolescence can be for a young boy and about the need to hide these feelings from others. However, instead of being able to use this understanding while still retaining his adult responsibility for the boys, he finds himself drawn into acting as though he were one of them. In his role as active participant in Ben's life, Marco loses the neutrality which he might have been able to use to help Ben out of his difficulties, or to negotiate effectively between Ben and his parents.

Not only can this kind of over-involvement lead to harm and embarrassment, trying to do too much can also inadvertently undermine the confidence of our clients, as the following example illustrates.

A nurse worried about one of her patients who had recently been diagnosed with diabetes. The woman had looked so frail and shocked by her diagnosis, that the nurse was concerned that she would be unable to maintain the self-administered injections of insulin that had been prescribed to control her illness. The nurse, who had always wished that she had given more time to her grandmother before she passed away, found herself overwhelmed by a strong need to make sure that her elderly patient was all right. As the woman lived nearby, the nurse took to popping in each day on her way to and from work. She spent the first few visits watching the woman awkwardly administer her own injections. Noticing her lack of competence with the syringe, the nurse finally took over from her. In effect, the nurse took over all administration of the insulin treatment and the diabetic patient took less and less responsibility for maintaining her health.

After some weeks of this arrangement, the nurse attended a day-long training session and was unable to visit the diabetic patient as before. When she arrived at her patient's home the following day, she was shocked to discover that the woman had not attempted to inject herself at all. The nurse quickly realized the potential danger of what she had been doing. It took some time and considerable support before the patient began to feel confident enough to take control of her own treatment. The nurse took to popping in to see her patient on a weekly basis to check for complications and to offer affirmation for the woman's attempts to help herself.

In this case, the nurse's experience with her own grandmother has made her very sensitive to the potential loneliness and isolation an elderly patient might feel. This sensitivity allows her to recognize her patient's need for care and to respond to it with the respect and compassion the woman deserves. In this situation, however, the nurse's guilt and regret about her own grandmother have made her want to provide more 'help' than is necessary. She offers so much help in fact, that she inadvertently leaves her client feeling helpless and unable to manage on her own.

It is not always easy to see the ways in which doing too much can sometimes be as much of a problem as doing nothing at all. In this example, however, the nurse was fortunately alerted to these potential problems by the obvious consequences of her actions. It may of course have been more useful and less alarming if she had come to this realization through an earlier process of reflection. Although it is often difficult to become aware of the meaning of our responses when we are caught up in the middle of a situation, it is helpful to keep thinking about our reactions – especially when they seem stronger or more intense than usual.

In the previous two examples, the nurse and the youth worker both seem to have been driven to offer some kind of practical help that far exceeded what was appropriate. In Ben's case, Marco's attempts to help him were clearly not effective. As for the diabetic patient, the results could have been even more awful. These are obviously fairly extreme examples, but it is important to think about some of the problems that can arise when our own emotional needs lead us to expect too much of ourselves as helpers. In most cases it is the care worker who ends up suffering the most as a result of unrealistic expectations of ourselves which arise out of the mixture of our own feelings and those of our clients.

The term *burnout* is appropriately used to describe what happens when people – most often those in the helping professions – try to take on more than they can realistically manage. The most frequent result of burnout is that people simply leave their jobs, resulting in a situation where human service organizations lose some of their best and most experienced workers. Long before this happens, however, care-workers who are taking on too much may find themselves feeling tired, disinterested in their work, and even angry and resentful of their clients who they feel they cannot effectively help. In some cases, frustration can lead to care-workers becoming angry and blaming those who they feel are responsible for their clients' distress.

Consider the example of a worker at a local centre for battered women who identifies very closely with many of her clients and who, on their behalf, becomes furious with the police for 'not doing their job'. Her anger is so intense that she refuses to have any contact with the police at all. While it is often true that the police services in this kind of situation are not always very helpful, this care-worker's particular way of expressing her anger is certainly of no help to her clients, who rely on the police to back up their legal injunctions.

In all of the cases we have described in this chapter, the feeling of connection that the care-workers have with their clients is both the source of their understanding and the basis of the difficulties that arise. Julia's intense sadness as she listens to a young girl struggling to hold things together as her mother lies dying of a terminal illness, certainly helps her to recognize how hard this situation is for Kershni. When Marco feels an overwhelming urge to help the wayward teenager, he is acting on his intuitive understanding of how vulnerable Ben really feels. Similarly, the nurse understands what a burden it is for an elderly person living on her own without any family support to manage a serious illness like diabetes. Even the angry worker at the centre for battered women probably uses her very emotional response to further her understanding of the experiences of the women she works with.

The care-workers' own experiences of how difficult these issues are to face, help them to recognize their emotional significance for their clients – a recognition that those less sensitive to the issues might easily have overlooked. Julia, for example, might easily have treated Kershni's cry for help as a realistic question about homework; Marco could have treated Ben as the delinquent teenager others regard him as; the nurse might easily have moved on to her next patient without 'seeing' the old lady's distress; the worker at the women's centre could have remained indifferent to the legitimate anger of her clients.

It is certainly no solution at all to suggest that care-workers simply cut themselves off from these important ways of understanding. They should rather keep thinking about what they are feeling in response to their clients, and why they might be feeling this way. Throughout this chapter we have used the idea of *self-reflection* to describe the ways in which people can think about their feelings in a helpful way. Self-reflection has many advantages for those of us who provide emotional care to others. Firstly, it helps us to know ourselves better in general, and to understand more about our own strengths and weaknesses in our work in particular. Secondly, it provides a means of working through some of the strong emotions that are evoked in care-work in order to prevent emotional distress and the long-term problems associated with burnout. Finally, it prevents us from acting impulsively or unhelpfully with our clients.

Self-reflection

It is not always easy to keep thinking when we are involved in the difficult process of trying to understand other people's needs and distress. Here are some ideas for how to build up a capacity for self-reflection.

- When working with clients, keep monitoring your own emotional responses and asking yourself where these feelings are coming from.
- Especially notice situations where your feelings become more intense than usual.
- Try to avoid jumping into action – give yourself the time to make sense of what you are feeling.
- No matter how busy your day – try to give yourself time to think about what you felt and why.
- Speak to colleagues about your work and how it makes you feel.
- Try to identify some of your strongest feelings and see whether they link to any experiences you've had in your life.
- Treat your own feelings with the same compassion and respect that you would give to your clients.
- Use your 'mistakes' as an opportunity to understand yourself – not to criticize yourself.

CHAPTER 2

Listening deeply

Listening carefully to what people say and don't say is extremely important for care-workers. It is essential to give people a chance to tell their own stories in their own words. As listeners, we also need to try and understand the clues people give us about some of their unspoken worries.

The idea of 'listening deeply' is taken from the book of this name by Howard Stein, published by Westview Press, Boulder, in 1994.

When we don't listen

Grace worked in a student advice office at a local technical college. She was new at her job and keen to prove herself able to manage the important responsibility of helping students adjust to college life. One aspect of her job was to assist students in making the right career choices. She wanted to be well-prepared for the range of questions students might want to put to her about different kinds of work and the sorts of subjects they might think of studying to equip themselves for the career they eventually chose. Fortunately she had started her job early on in the year and had a few weeks to get herself ready before the students began their term. She used her time productively and scoured the library for helpful resource books and even visited some local employment agencies to make sure her information was up to date. When the students started to trickle in at the start of the new year, Grace found herself easily able to answer their questions and felt rather pleased with herself for being 'so on top of things'. After several weeks of this kind of experience she was feeling quite competent in her new job.

Around about this time Grace received a phone call from a young man who sounded very unsure about whether or not he needed to see her. He said he was having some problems at college but wasn't sure if he was calling the right place to get help. "If it's problems with college, you're definitely in the right place!" Grace assured him cheerfully. He seemed about to say something else but she quickly told him that she had an open appointment the next day and that she would see him then. She put down the phone and entered his appointment time into her neatly kept diary.

The next day the young student, whose name was Thabo, arrived late for his appointment. Grace felt rather irritated. She had squeezed him in between two other interviews and thought that his behaviour was rather inconsiderate. Thabo came into the room slowly and sat down, keeping his head turned away from Grace who was sorting out her reference notes on her desk. "Well," said Grace, her irritation making her slightly more brisk than usual, "what can I do for you?" Thabo spoke hesitantly and began by saying that he had some problems with his course. He was about to say something else when Grace interrupted him. "What course are you doing?" she asked, wanting to make sure her facts were correct so that she could advise him properly. He replied that he was doing business management. "Well," said Grace, "luckily it's early in the year – you have quite a range of options to choose from." She showed Thabo the directory of courses she had opened in front of him and pointed out some likely alternatives for a student with his background. Throughout this discussion, Thabo remained largely silent, giving only essential information when asked. He nodded his head now and again to show he understood Grace's suggestions. Close to the end of the half hour set aside for the interview, Grace asked Thabo if he was any clearer about what he wanted to do. He seemed very uncertain and as they had little time left, Grace decided to offer him an appointment time the following day so that they could complete their discussion. Thabo said goodbye politely and agreed that he would return for their next appointment.

Later that afternoon, Grace took a phone call from a warden at the local students' residence. Apologizing for not having contacted her earlier, the warden said she was phoning because she was worried about one of the students who lived in the residence where she worked. She explained that the student was a young man who had seemed very unhappy in the past weeks. From the little she knew, she was aware that he had recently heard about the death of his brother in a car accident. He seemed, since then, to have lost interest in his studies and was apparently thinking about giving up his course. The warden felt that the student had the potential to do well and was hoping that if he just had a chance to talk about how he was feeling, there might be an opportunity to prevent him from dropping out completely. She asked if Grace would be prepared to see him and speak to him for a bit. If the problem was serious, she suggested that Grace could perhaps refer him on to the student counselling service for some additional help.

Grace was pleased to be asked to speak to the student, feeling that this was a part of her job she had not yet had the opportunity to develop properly. She agreed to see the student and asked for his name so that she would know who he was when he phoned or stopped by. The warden said his name was Thabo and Grace was surprised to realize that he was the same student who had already called and seen her earlier that day. She explained to the warden that she had already seen him but that she had not been told about his additional problems – only that he was unhappy with his course. Fortunately, Grace said, she had another appointment with him the following day and would now be in a better position to explore these issues with him.

On putting down the phone, Grace felt puzzled at first. Why, she wondered, had Thabo not been able to confide in her? As she retraced their conversation in her head, however, Grace began to realize that in fact it might have been *she* who had decided that Thabo's main problem was with his course. She recognized that she hadn't given him the opportunity to talk about anything else that might have been bothering him. In fact, the more she thought about it, the more uncomfortable she felt about the way in which she had tried to hurry him into making a decision about an alternative course. She realized that this was more than likely not his concern at all. For the rest of the afternoon, Grace continued to think about what had happened during her conversation with Thabo. She became increasingly aware that she had been distracted by her own irritation and was so busy 'listening' to her own interests and concerns that she had not really listened to Thabo at all.

When Thabo arrived for his appointment the following day Grace was careful to begin the session with an apology. "I didn't really give you a chance to say what you wanted from me yesterday. Let's take a bit more time today and perhaps you can tell me what it is you would really like help with," she said.

There was an uncomfortable silence after Grace spoke, but a few minutes later Thabo looked up and said, "I just feel like everything is messed up at the moment. I don't think it would matter what course I was doing – I just don't think I'm coping ...". Grace nodded, but having learned her lesson from the previous day, she did not interrupt but rather waited for him to tell her his story in his own words.

Becoming a good listener

Listening is a fundamental skill in many areas of work. Without being able to listen to people, to really understand what it is that they mean and what their needs are, we are unable to help them, educate them, guide them, or serve them. For those of us who work as carers, listening is often a vital part of our jobs and, in itself, is thought to help people resolve their problems and to feel better about themselves. The experience of really being listened to and understood is often exactly what many of the people we work with lack in their lives. To have someone pay careful attention to what they say and take it seriously, helps to make them feel worthwhile and gives them an important space in which to make sense of what it is that they feel and think.

Being a good listener is not always easy and there are many things that seem to get in the way of our really hearing or understanding what it is that people want to say to us. Many of us tend to think of listening as something that we do automatically, without really thinking about it. The reality though, is that for most of us, even when we appear to be engrossed in conversation with someone, we are not always listening to what they say. Like Grace, many of us may find ourselves distracted by our own concerns and by our assumptions that we know what it is that the other person is going to say.

In the above example, Grace's irritation with Thabo's lateness may have got in the way of her wanting to listen to what he said from the start. When we are angry with people it is much more likely that we will not listen to them properly. Ironically, Grace's concerns about knowing how to do her job well, also seem to have got in the way of her making a space in which to hear what Thabo had to say to her. Anxious about managing her new job, Grace placed a lot of pressure on herself to have all the answers for the students who came to her for help. She was so busy thinking about what she needed to know and all the information she had to give Thabo, that it was hard for her to stop and really listen to him. It was fortunate that she made the second appointment with Thabo and so was able to really hear about what was actually bothering him.

In her second interview with Thabo, Grace was able to properly prepare the way for real listening. The most important part of doing this is to give someone the space in which to talk – in their own words and at their own pace. If we do not allow this, what we end up with is a situation in which we hear only the echoes of our own questions. It took some courage for Grace to apologize for her mistake and then wait in silence for Thabo to be able to begin talking.

For most of us, sitting in silence is very difficult. We are taught to believe that silence during a conversation means that the people involved either do not like each other, or have some other equally uncomfortable reason for not wishing to talk to one another. While this might very well be the case, it is also true that in many instances when people are silent, they are simply thinking about what it is they want to say. Of course this is more likely to happen when people are getting ready to talk about something that is really important to them. We often imagine, because of our own nervousness about silence, that we need to jump in straight away with questions to help the other person to talk. The problem with launching in with rapid-fire questioning too soon is that we may, in the phrasing of our questions, prevent the other person from really expressing what they want to say.

We saw in this example how Grace's apparently 'helpful' questions about Thabo's course actually prevented him from talking about his real problems. Even with the information from the warden to guide her, Grace could easily have made the same mistake in the second interview. She might have decided, for example, to begin by saying something like, "I believe you have been upset by your brother's death. Tell me what happened and how it made you feel." This kind of questioning might seem logical given the circumstances of the referral, but it can also create problems and limit the person's potential responses – Thabo might not yet be ready to talk about this sensitive area so soon into his relationship with a relative stranger for instance, or this might not in fact be the main problem he is struggling with, but merely be what the warden has assumed is his difficulty. This kind of questioning could make Thabo feel that this is the only issue he is 'allowed' to discuss and it might stop him from talking about his most pressing problem, which, for all Grace knows, could be about a girlfriend who has recently left him. The point is, we cannot know any of this until we allow the person to speak to us and to describe their experiences to us in a way that makes sense to them.

Now of course it would be equally difficult for someone to talk to us if we remained stonily silent throughout their discussion. Importantly, Grace does not do this. Instead, she starts off with a question – an open-ended kind of question that is intended to give Thabo the go-ahead to talk (as opposed to a question designed to draw out any particular kind of information). In her conversation with him, it is likely that she would ask other questions as well, but hopefully these would not interrupt the flow of Thabo's story or introduce ideas that reflect Grace's concerns above his own. Rather, it may be helpful if she were to encourage him to continue talking by simply nodding or showing in other non-verbal ways that she is still listening. Counsellors also often find it useful to repeat back to the person the main things they have understood from what has been said to them. This is sometimes called *reflection* because the technique is a metaphorical mirror that shows the person what they have said. This can be helpful because it gives the listener a chance to check out whether they have heard or understood correctly, and also reassures the person talking that what they have said has been understood accurately. After some time of listening to the person, it might be useful to ask some direct questions to clarify your understanding, but this should preferably only happen once the person has had a chance to say what they wanted to say. Many counselling manuals will provide guidelines for how to respond when someone is talking, for example by making eye-contact or sitting in a certain way. In general, though, each of us has to find our own way of being with someone that feels comfortable and right for us and the situation in which we are in. If you are a care-worker, what is most often required of you is to really try to listen and hear what your clients say to you.

Listening beyond the words

Allowing someone to talk is only the beginning of listening, however. It is quite possible to give someone the freedom to tell you what they are thinking without taking in a single word that they say. Many of us do this in social conversations. As we listen to someone telling us their bit of news, our minds often dart ahead to think of an entertaining anecdote we might tell next. It is sometimes useful to experiment and test ourselves with how much we have actually taken in and remembered of what a person has said to us. For many of us, if we are not actually concentrating hard at listening, we may find that there is in fact very little we could repeat about what we have been told. It is helpful to try and really focus on what someone is telling us in a way that helps us draw out and understand the main meaning they are trying to get across.

It is often difficult to understand what people have to say even when they are allowed to tell a story in their own words. It is not unusual for people to spend a bit of time umming and aahing in the beginning before they start talking. Many of us also go round and round a bit while we try and work out what we want to say – often giving all sorts of unnecessary bits of detail along the way. This is especially obvious when people are feeling nervous or upset as they often might be when they are talking in the context of a helping relationship. Part of what we as helpers need to do is provide a space in which people can, through talking, begin to make sense of what they are thinking and how they are feeling. It will usually take some time before it is clear to us – and even to the person themselves – what it is they need or want. The main thing here is to be patient enough to allow your and their understanding to grow gradually.

Our understanding of what people mean, however, is not just taken from the words that they speak, but also from how they show their feelings about what they are saying. To use a very simple example, a person rolling their eyes while saying, "That's a brilliant idea!" would mean something very different from what their words suggest. Similarly, we all know that someone can say "that's fine" in a way that clearly shows that it's not fine at all. All of us quite intuitively make sense of the non-verbal clues that help us to understand the meaning of the words that we hear. We put them together in a way that helps us to listen not just to what someone says to us – but also what these things mean to them.

If we look carefully at the example of Grace and Thabo again, we will see that there are all kinds of clues that tell us helpful things about how Thabo is feeling about his situation. If Grace had been 'listening' to all these things, she may have realized much earlier on that Thabo was worried about something. The very first contact we have with someone is often quite revealing. When Thabo makes his initial phone call he sounds quite uncertain about whether he has contacted the right place for help. In terms of the spoken communication here, it would have been helpful had Grace asked him to explain briefly what he needed. However, his very uncertainty is also an indication of how he is feeling more generally. When someone is feeling unhappy and unconfident they often doubt their own actions and choices in the way that Thabo appears to. Had Grace picked up on this when listening to him on the phone, she could have started to develop an understanding of him that she would have been able to test out more fully in the interview.

There were also other early clues as to what Thabo was feeling. He arrived late for his first interview. In fact, Grace does use this piece of information in her understanding, but she unfortunately only imagines that it reflects inconsiderateness on Thabo's part. While this is perfectly possible, Grace should nevertheless have considered that people are often late for other reasons. It is common, for example, for people who are unsure about whether or not they want to attend something, to be late for it. It is also not unusual for people who are depressed to struggle to find the energy to get to an appointment on time. Similarly, people whose lives are chaotic for whatever reason might also find it difficult to keep appointment times. Both Grace and Thabo would have benefited had Grace thought about some of these things in preparation for her meeting with Thabo. People also reveal a great deal about how they are feeling from the way that they carry their bodies. When someone is cheerful they may bounce along, while a person who is sad often looks like they are indeed carrying a heavy burden across their shoulders. Thabo's slowness and the way he avoided eye contact with Grace could have alerted her early on to his sadness and may have helped her to know what to expect from him.

There are, in fact, many situations where we rely more on what people do or how they look than on what they say in order to make sense of what they are trying to tell us. A colleague who slams a door after a meeting tells us very clearly that he is angry, or more specifically, that he does not agree with the decision made by the group. When a woman's eyes fill with tears during a sad movie, we do not have to be told that it has touched her own sadness to know this. When only a few school children turn up to hear the headmaster give his annual lecture we can probably safely assume that he is not popular among them. It is through observing these wordless communications that we are able to make sense of many different situations even when we are not told openly what is going on. Care-workers not only need to develop their capacity to listen closely and attentively to what people say, but also to observe closely what they do.

This is of course particularly important in situations where people are unwilling or unable to put their thoughts and feelings into words. Many people may at first be reluctant to speak to a stranger about their situation and initially we may have to rely a great deal on the subtle clues that they give us through their behaviour. Lots of people also struggle to talk openly about things that feel very painful for them and it is not uncommon to find someone with tears in their eyes insisting that they only have a bit of a cold. Of course we can never know without asking whether or not our interpretation of what we see is accurate, but noticing these things is often a good place to start the process of trying to understand someone.

Care-workers who work with young children are often very used to looking carefully at how the children behave in order to try and make sense of what they are feeling or thinking. Consider the following incident which is an example of how useful this kind of observation can be.

A playschool teacher noticed one of the three-year-olds in her class playing with the baby doll at the back of the room. The teacher was at first rather alarmed to observe Tanvi, a normally very gentle child, picking up the doll roughly and throwing it on the ground. The teacher stood fairly close by and watched Tanvi repeating this action again and again. Finally, the teacher approached her and said gently that she thought Tanvi must be rather cross with the baby doll to throw her on the ground that way. Tanvi replied that the doll was naughty and that there was no place for her inside the house. "She has to sleep outside in the cold!" Tanvi said.

The teacher made no further comment, but later, when Tanvi's mother came to fetch her, she called her aside and asked her whether she knew of anything that could be upsetting Tanvi at the moment. Without hesitation, Tanvi's mother said that Tanvi had seemed angry about her new baby brother sleeping in her parents' room where they had put him temporarily so that they could keep an eye on him through a mild illness. "I think," said Tanvi's mother, "that she is feeling that we love the baby more than we love her. She says it's unfair that the baby can sleep with us when she has to sleep all alone." The teacher passed on to Tanvi's mother her observation that the little girl did indeed seem to feel a bit left out and angry with her brother because of this. She pointed out that this was perfectly normal behaviour but that Tanvi might need some reassurance from her parents that they still loved her in the same way.

This conversation helped the teacher to begin to make sense of Tanvi's strange behaviour. The next day she was very careful to give Tanvi some little jobs around the classroom that helped her to feel special. Tanvi seemed to respond well to this extra attention and soon stopped playing so roughly with the baby doll. In fact, later in the week, the teacher noticed Tanvi carrying the baby doll gently, patting it and saying softly, "Don't cry. It's all right."

Young children do not communicate primarily in words. They show us what they feel and think through their behaviour and also through the way they play. In this example, the pre-school teacher uses a combination of her observation of Tanvi's play and a conversation with Tanvi's mother to help her make sense of what Tanvi might be experiencing, and to help both parties to deal with it. It was important that the teacher took the time to watch carefully and see what it was that Tanvi was doing, even when she did not immediately understand what it might mean. Later she gets some background information from Tanvi's mother and is able to work out that Tanvi, in playing so roughly with the doll, was trying to let out some of her cross feelings towards the baby brother who made her feel excluded from her parents' affections. In response, the teacher very sensitively gives Tanvi a bit of extra attention to help her feel that she is special and this, along with her parents' awareness of how Tanvi might be feeling, seems to help her get over her jealousy.

Listening in groups

Up until now we have been talking about the different ways of communicating and listening that take place between two people. Many care-workers, however, often have to work with people in groups. Of course in a group context it remains just as important to listen carefully to what people are saying and to look for clues to what they are feeling in their behaviour and expressions, as it is between two people. But there are also some additional things that are helpful to the listening process in groups. Consider the following example.

Fathima worked at a local community centre where she facilitated a support group for men who were struggling to get their lives back together after their release from prison. The aim of the group was to give the men an opportunity to talk together about their difficulties in readjusting to family life, finding jobs, and generally fitting back into the community. The idea was that they would be able to support each other and offer each other advice from their personal experiences. Fathima felt that her role was really just to get the men together and not to play an active part in deciding what they should talk about. She felt strongly that the group belonged not to her, but to the men themselves. Part of her reason for thinking this was that she recognized that the men had been so put down by their prison experience that they needed to rediscover their own ability to control their lives. The group, however, did not develop as she had hoped.

Within a few sessions it was clear that there were two men who were outspoken and sometimes even aggressive. They interrupted others while they were talking and their ideas dominated any discussion. Other members of the group became more and more silent as they listened to the views of these two. The group seemed to become an increasingly tense and uncomfortable place to be. Fathima's concern intensified when she noticed that some of the quieter members of the group were no longer attending the sessions. She felt that she had to do something to ensure that everyone had a space to talk, and to help people feel comfortable with one another. She gathered her courage and decided to confront the issue directly in the group.

She began the next group session by pointing out that she had noticed that not everyone seemed to get a chance to talk in the group and that she was worried about this situation. Her comment was met initially by silence and then one of the two talkative members of the group responded by saying that he had not noticed the problem. Fathima said that while she respected his opinion, she was certain that this was not the only view in the group. One by one she asked the others how they felt. Although some members seemed to have difficulty expressing themselves, most acknowledged that they would like to be able to talk more easily in the group. A few were brave enough to admit that they resented the dominance of the two talkative members. Others pointed out that they were worried about talking freely in the group in case other group members told everyone what they said.

Forced by Fathima's strategy to listen to what others in the group had to say, the two over-talkative members sat silently. Finally, one spoke up and apologized sincerely for not having let other people speak. He said that he had very few friends, and no one he knew would tell him honestly if he did something they didn't like. From then on the tension eased and the group, led by Fathima, agreed that they needed to develop some ground rules that would enable everyone to talk. They decided that each person needed to take responsibility for saying what they wanted to say – but that when anyone started to talk they would be listened to respectfully until they had finished. They also agreed not to talk to outsiders about what was discussed in the group.

As this example shows, talking and listening in groups can be particularly tricky. Whenever any group comes together there will be some people who find it easy to say what they think and others who find it difficult to express themselves. Although we cannot expect everyone to speak in exactly the same kind of way, it is sometimes necessary, as Fathima found, to silence some members of a group temporarily in order to make a space for others to talk. For many care-workers the role of listener is a much more comfortable one than the more assertive role that Fathima had to play in this group. She was fortunately able to find the courage to use her authority in the group to address a problem that would otherwise have got in the way of all members being able to use the group effectively. Importantly though, her role in this regard was temporary and having pointed out the problem, she quickly hands it back for the group to decide what rules they need to help facilitate everyone speaking.

It is not just care-workers who need to learn how to listen. In the above example, Fathima facilitates this skill among the men by sharing her observation of what is happening in the group. Similar observations can be used helpfully among colleagues in staff meetings and discussions where it frequently happens that only some voices are heard. Many people, especially those whose trust in others has been damaged, may be afraid to risk talking to others. They may worry about whether they can trust people not to gossip about them or use the information they get to hurt them in some way. This kind of feeling is often very strong in groups where it is unlikely that you will get to know everyone equally well before you start talking. In groups it is very helpful to begin with some agreement on 'ground rules' like respect and confidentiality that protect the safety of the members to talk.

A safe space for listening

Talking and listening take place all the time in a wide variety of settings. We talk and listen to people in the corridors as we walk past them, in the streets outside our houses, in lecture halls, and in classrooms. It is respectful in all these situations to listen carefully and to try to understand what it is that people are trying to tell us. In some situations, though, we may need slightly more time and a 'safer' place in which to be able to make sense of something important someone is trying to say.

As care-workers, many of us will be approached by people needing specific help with an emotional difficulty. In these cases it is often not suitable to talk outside in a public place where the conversation can easily be overheard or interrupted. Most people would feel more comfortable talking in a place where there is some privacy, some quiet, and a sense that they have the time that they need to say what they want to say. Although it is not always possible in every work setting, it is really helpful to have one space that can be used for these kinds of conversations. Because most people feel a bit anxious about talking about how they are feeling, they are easily distracted by a ringing telephone or a badly timed knock on the door. People also, quite naturally, feel sensitive about revealing themselves to someone and may be on the lookout for clues that you are uninterested in what they are saying. A counsellor who encourages a client to tell her what she is really feeling and then glances at her watch, should not be surprised if the client is hesitant to open up to her. Similarly, a teacher who interrupts his conversation with a distressed pupil so that he can have a long chat with one of his colleagues, is unlikely to receive a confidence.

What most people need when they talk to someone is a protected space in which they can think and in which they feel that someone is listening carefully and attentively to them. Some counselling manuals write about the importance of placing chairs in different kinds of ways, but this matters less than making sure it's an environment in which you and the person you are talking to can feel comfortable. With adults, for example, it sometimes works best to have two chairs that don't quite face each other, and which are separated by a low coffee table rather than a desk. Many children, however, would associate this kind of seating arrangement with an unwelcome visit to the principal's office. With a child it may be much more appropriate to talk in a secluded section of the playground where the child can play while he or she talks. Teenagers might also feel more comfortable talking while engaged in some kind of task because they then do not have to feel the embarrassment of someone staring at them while waiting for them to say something.

As a care-worker, the ability to listen thoughtfully to what someone is trying to tell you about what they have experienced or how they are feeling is invaluable. Many of us worry too much about what we will do if someone approaches us for help with an emotional problem. We are concerned that we might somehow say the wrong thing or not be able to give what is needed. In very many situations, however, all that is required of us is to listen. Many of us know first hand how good it feels to be heard and how comforting it is when it seems that we have been understood. Many of the people with whom we work can benefit from the experience of talking to someone who allows them the unique opportunity of making sense of how they feel and finding out what it is they are thinking.

Listening

- Recognize the value of being able to talk and having someone listen.
- Understand how hard it is to talk about things that are important.
- Make a space for people to say what they feel and think without interruption.
- Let people find their own words with which to talk, and to say things in their own time.
- Concentrate on what is being said rather than on what you need to do or say.
- Listen to the unspoken messages in people's expressions and in what they do.
- Find a safe place to talk in.

CHAPTER 3

Coping with feelings

An important part of being able to help others cope with their feelings relates to how well we are able to cope with our own. Whenever we work with people, in whatever capacity, emotions are evoked in us. These emotions have to do with our own responses to the work, as well as with the feelings that the people we are working with communicate to us. Understanding and coping with our feelings is the first step in helping others to cope with theirs.

Thinking about feelings

Our roles often require that we go one step beyond the listening we described in Chapter 2. We help people make decisions, understand new material, meet the requirements of their jobs, or come to terms with difficulties. Part of this assistance involves helping people to manage the different emotions that are stirred up by their activities. For a manager this might mean helping staff with feelings of demotivation. For a teacher it might involve helping children who are anxious about learning.

Counselling proves a useful arena to explore these processes. Counselling is all about listening, communication, and helping people to understand and begin to think about difficult feelings. Let's look at an example of counselling.

Coming to terms with the sadness and fear of being HIV positive

The setting is an HIV clinic that provides tertiary care for patients diagnosed as HIV positive. Anant, a nurse, has completed a training course in HIV counselling. A large part of his work involves pre- and post-test counselling, but occasionally clients ask for counselling for other sorts of issues.

The first meeting

An HIV positive man, Tsepho, arrived at the clinic for follow-up tests. He asked to speak to one of the counsellors. Anant went to talk to Tsepho.

"Why is it that you want to talk?" Anant asked.

"I'm worried because I haven't seen my children for weeks. My wife left me a couple of months ago and has moved far away." After a brief silence, Tsepho continued, "My previous wife also left me. I have three children from my first marriage, and two from the second. I miss them all very much."

Tsepho spent a long time talking to Anant about fatherhood, recalling several events in his life with his families. "The problem is that at the moment I can't be part of my children's lives. You know, experience has taught me that life is very hard, and I accept that, but I miss my children very much."

Listening to Tsepho, Anant felt anxious at first, wondering if Tsepho was in some sort of crisis. He felt calmer as Tsepho began talking about the problem of not being able to see his children, and started thinking to himself that given that Tsepho's concerns were not about being HIV positive, perhaps Tsepho should be talking to a social worker concerning access to his children. He felt touched, however, as Tsepho spoke sadly about his memories of the children. As Tsepho was talking, Anant suddenly noticed Tsepho's wrists, which appeared to be very thin.

Anant was startled. It occurred to him that Tsepho had developed full-blown AIDS. In that moment, he lost concentration and found it difficult to think. He had to work hard to focus on what Tsepho was saying.

As Anant battled to regain his composure, Tsepho continued talking in a somewhat distracted way about his family. Anant tried very hard to follow what Tsepho was saying. "Pull yourself together," he silently admonished himself. He tried to remind himself that as a counsellor he was supposed to reflect feelings. He realized that Tsepho was a very sad man. "This has made you very sad," he said to Tsepho.

"Yes, I am," Tsepho said with tears welling up in his eyes. "I'd like to find another wife, but no one will have me. It's hard to have this sickness. People see you as contagious. I'm sleeping very badly. I toss and turn and have bad dreams. I don't go out very much and I feel very alone." Tsepho looked at Anant and said, "You know, the last time I came to the clinic I got lost, but this time I found the right place. I feel that you understand me. What's your name again?"

"Anant."

Tsepho sat quietly for a while, lost to his own thoughts. Then he said, "The last Anant I knew of was that famous cricket player. I really liked the way he played."

As Tsepho spoke, Anant felt very sad. He was acutely aware of how painful it was for Tsepho to have lost contact with his family.

It was time for the meeting to end.

"Anant," Tsepho said, "thank you. It does a person good to talk. I think a weight has been lifted off my shoulders."

After the meeting

After the meeting, Anant walked through to the staffroom where he found a nurse and a doctor discussing a patient. He overheard the doctor saying that the patient was too demanding. Anant suddenly felt very angry with the doctor. "Don't you think he's probably scared?" he interjected rather aggressively. The doctor looked startled and taken aback. At home that night Anant found it hard to sleep. Tsepho was very much on his mind; his thin arms, the children he hadn't seen in a long time, his sadness and loneliness.

Over the next few days, Anant found himself thinking about Tsepho. Four days after his meeting with Tsepho, Anant was chatting with a colleague. He related how he had found the conversation with Tsepho painful, and that he had felt thrown during their meeting. "I didn't know what to say, it was so sad," he said. "Then I heard Doctor Lin talking about that guy in Ward four. She sounded so callous. I couldn't believe Lin would talk like that. I was just so mad."

His colleague thought for a bit. "Maybe Lin was also thrown by her patient? Maybe she didn't know how to deal with her situation either?" he suggested.

Anant felt soothed by this comment. He had not considered that the doctor might also have been struggling with something difficult. Anant thought about the many painful consequences of becoming HIV positive, and how hard an adjustment it must be to make. He thought again about how hard things must be for Tsepho.

The second meeting

A week later, Anant was informed that Tsepho had returned to the clinic for more tests and wished to speak with him. As Anant walked towards the waiting room, he found himself remembering the last meeting and felt overwhelmed by the same sense of being unable to think. This time though, he thought about this feeling. Tsepho's situation was so painful, he acknowledged to himself, how could he expect to know how to think about it? It occurred to him that Tsepho must be feeling something similar, and probably didn't know how to think about it either. By the time Anant greeted Tsepho, he was feeling more composed.

In this second meeting, Tsepho was very emotional, saying that he felt confused and didn't know which way to turn. Anant recognized that Tsepho's sense of turmoil was an amplified version of what he had been feeling earlier, and that Tsepho was very afraid. Anant said to Tsepho, "You're dealing with something extremely difficult and painful. You must not know what to do or feel. I guess you must be really scared."

Tsepho began to cry. "I might have to move. I can't afford to stay where I am anymore. I've been putting off dealing with it. I just don't know what to do. I'm really scared and I don't know where I'm going to stay." Anant listened to Tsepho quietly. After a while Tsepho began to calm. "I've tried to keep up a brave face," he said. "I haven't told anyone how scared I am."

Anant thought to himself that given the anguish that Tsepho was going through, it was no wonder that he felt unable to tackle his accommodation problem. With this recognition in mind, he began to ask Tsepho questions about his options, and the two began to explore the problem.

How can we understand the emotional process that has happened between Tsepho and Anant? Let us take a closer look at the two meetings, and at what was happening for Tsepho and Anant.

The first meeting

Tsepho came to the clinic battling very difficult feelings including loss, anger, despair, helplessness, and confusion. He was finding it very difficult to cope with these feelings, which were in a sense unbearable for him. It seems that part of the way in which he had been coping was by concentrating on the things that had been positive in his life – his relationship with his children, and his idea of himself as a good father. Tsepho spent a lot of time talking about this in the first meeting.

At first, both Anant and Tsepho understood Tsepho's struggle as one that involved the loss of his children. Issues and feelings concerning his illness were put to one side. It seems that Tsepho had been putting these feelings aside during his daily life as well, in order to cope with them. What Tsepho was able to do, however, was hold onto a sense of himself as a capable and responsible father. This allowed him a sense of being able to control what was happening in his life, at a time when he was feeling very out of control indeed.

It is very common for people to cope in this way because it provides them with a sense of order and a link to a time in the past when they felt strong and able to influence events. One wonders if, in fact, Tsepho's life was really as he remembered it prior to his HIV-positive diagnosis. We might speculate that his life had had its share of pain and problems, suggested by the fact that he had lost two wives. What is important, however, is that Anant and Tsepho came to an initial common understanding of what was troubling Tsepho, and that for both of them, this understanding involved putting away the concerns to do with HIV/AIDS.

A turning point

Later in the meeting, a striking thing happens. Anant suddenly becomes aware of Tsepho's very thin wrists, which indicate to him that Tsepho probably has AIDS. At this sudden reminder that Tsepho is ill, Anant becomes very anxious and finds it hard to think. He battles to regain composure. Because Tsepho's illness was something that the two had put to one side up to this point in the meeting, Anant found himself struggling to deal with the thought that Tsepho was, in fact, very ill. While Anant was occupied with these thoughts, Tsepho continued to talk distractedly about his family.

Anant's loss of composure was related to him becoming conscious of very powerful and complex feelings within himself. These were very similar to, but less intense than, those with which Tsepho was struggling – very high levels of anxiety and a sense of being unable to think. As Anant struggled to contain himself, he realized just how sad Tsepho was. This realization enabled him, for the first time in the conversation, to make a comment to Tsepho about how he must be feeling.

Anant had become aware of feelings that Tsepho had not been able to manage by himself, and had come to understand them. His comment about how sad Tsepho must be feeling made some sense of things for Tsepho. It was an understanding and empathetic comment that allowed Tsepho to talk about his sadness and loneliness, and also about how difficult it was to have this illness because of other people's reactions to it and him as a result.

At the end of the meeting, Tsepho says that he got lost the last time he came to the clinic, but that this time he had found the right place. He then likens Anant to a sports star whom he admires. It seems that he is trying to tell Anant that he feels understood. He leaves the meeting with a feeling of having been unburdened, while Anant seems to have taken on some of Tsepho's load.

Understanding Anant's feelings

After his meeting with Tsepho, when Anant overhears Doctor Lin's conversation, he is angered and disappointed and his aggression towards the doctor startles her. It seems that Anant was left with a mixture of emotions after his meeting with Tsepho. Their conversation was on his mind the whole day and he thought through it at home that night and battled to sleep. Anant was trying to understand something. He talked to his colleague about the interaction with the doctor and with Tsepho. His colleague's comment about Doctor Lin perhaps not knowing how to deal with her patient helps Anant to realize something about his own response to Tsepho. He realizes that there is something that he has been struggling to understand about Tsepho's experience.

When he sees Tsepho next, he once again feels very anxious and unable to think. This time, however, he is able to focus on how hard it must be for Tsepho to manage his problems. When Anant offers this understanding, Tsepho begins to cry. For the first time, he is able to admit just how scared he has been feeling. Anant uses this understanding to be helpful, initiating some discussion and beginning to explore Tsepho's potential options.

Containment: communicating emotion

How do we understand how Anant helped Tsepho with his painful feelings? We have followed the emotional journey that Anant underwent in order to be helpful to Tsepho. This story is not unique. At various times all people have feelings or thoughts that are difficult for them to manage by themselves. People may feel that things are too much for them, that they are not coping, or that they have become 'stuck'. Equally, people may feel demotivated, blocked, or unfulfilled. At these times people may try to rid themselves of these feelings, or to come to terms with them. They may also have an expectation that others will help them with these troubles. In psychological terms, the process of helping someone think through unbearable thoughts and feelings is described by the term *containment*.

What is containment?

Imagine each of us has a jug that is used to store or contain our feelings. Sometimes our jugs can't hold our feelings – perhaps we don't understand them, or perhaps there are too many feelings to fit into the jug. At times like this, it's useful to pour some of our feelings into another jug. That way, they can be contained somewhere else till we are ready to get them back. When we share something with someone else, it's as though we are pouring some of our difficult feelings from our jug into theirs. Let's consider how this process happens between a baby and her mother.

Children and babies are constantly confronted with experiences that are unmanageable to them, such as feelings of hunger, anxiety and so on. Children turn to their parents to help them make sense of these experiences and to meet their needs. For example, a baby begins to have a sensation of being hungry, but is as yet unable to put it together in his or her mind that the sensation means that he or she is hungry. The baby begins to cry. It is as though the baby's jug is now full. The mother becomes aware of the baby's distress and thinks about what it is that is causing the baby to be upset. The mother is likely to have felt something of the child's distress, and in part uses this feeling to understand what the child is feeling. She thinks, "Oh, she's hungry," and gives the baby food. The mother has taken some of the baby's feelings into her jug, done something with the feelings while she has held them, and then has given them back little by little to her child, pouring them back into her baby's jug slowly so that they don't spill over.

The baby has a sense of having been understood and as this process is repeated over time, the baby begins to be able to identify his or her own feelings and what they mean. The baby begins to have an ability to think about and manage emotions. The metaphor of containment thus works as follows: the baby puts the unmanageable or unbearable feelings (the feelings to be contained) into the mother's mind (the jug, the container). The mother, being a container, processes, thinks about, or digests the feelings and returns them to the child in a manageable form, for example through soothing words and actions (calming the baby and offering food). In this process, the baby comes to feel contained. Put another way, the child is held in the mother's mind.

A child develops the ability to cope with feelings by having repeated experiences of seemingly unmanageable thoughts and feelings being contained by a parent, who helps him or her to think them through. The baby then comes to internalize a container and is able to think for him or herself. In a way, the baby develops her own jug, one that is strong enough to hold her feelings. The child is then able to name, understand, and think through feelings. When the child is confronted with the unfamiliar, he or she will have some capacity to cope with the feelings evoked on his or her own. The child is developing a degree of independence, or the ability to be self-contained. There will, however, be periods when the child is unable to manage certain feelings (such as being separated from his or her parents for instance) and then, in a case of 'two steps forward and one back', the child will again feel unable to cope and will need a containing and comforting helping mind.

Cathy's maths problem

Nine-year-old Cathy was battling to do a difficult maths problem. It was something new, something that she hadn't learned before. She couldn't seem to understand how to do it and started to feel frustrated. Noticing her obvious frustration, her teacher walked up to her. "What's wrong?" she asked.

"It's too hard! I can't do it!" Cathy said in a discouraged tone.

"Yes, I know it's hard. These are tough problems. Tell me what you have been doing."

Cathy explained how she'd been trying to solve the problem and her teacher was able to help her understand. Her teacher's response made Cathy feel understood. By taking on some of Cathy's distress, her teacher gave Cathy some breathing space that allowed her to feel a little stronger and to think more clearly.

Throughout our lives we are all confronted by experiences that overwhelm our capacity to manage and think about them. These include experiences of falling ill, of loss, of trauma or disappointment. Even positive experiences can at times seem overwhelming, such as the news of an outstanding achievement. Stress researchers have long shown that both positive and negative occurrences can be experienced as stressful. These experiences evoke strong feelings in us, including the feeling of being helpless and unable to think. We are then confronted by feelings that we are unable to contain by ourselves. At times like this, people sometimes turn to others for help. These times can occur at any stage in one's life and depend, in part, on the nature of the experience, what it means for the person, as well as where the person is at in his or her life at the time of the event. Tsepho had come to such a time in his life.

Anant and Tsepho: applying the model of containment

The notion of containment is useful in explaining the emotional communication between Anant and Tsepho. Tsepho placed feelings that were too much for him (his fear, sadness, and inability to think about his situation) into the container provided by Anant's mind. Tsepho felt literally that he had unburdened himself and, as we have seen, Anant felt like he had taken something onto his shoulders. Tsepho's story stirred up powerful feelings in Anant who had to work hard to think through and process these feelings during their meetings. We saw at least two examples of this. In the first meeting, Anant needed to work hard to regain composure and in so doing, realized how sad Tsepho was. On the second occasion, he realized how scared Tsepho was, and how hard it was for Tsepho to think through his experience. Anant returned these feelings to Tsepho in a more manageable form through his reflections ("This has made you very sad." and "You're dealing with something extremely difficult and painful. You must not know what to do or feel. I guess you must be really scared."). This helped Tsepho to feel understood, and enabled him to begin to think about his feelings.

Our feelings as a source of information

Whenever we work with people some form of communication of emotions will occur. We are likely to have a range of emotional responses to the people we work with, the stories they tell, the way in which they behave, as well as the groups in which we find ourselves. The feelings we have are clues to what others are experiencing and help us make sense of their responses. Two people with similar concerns can evoke very different feelings. The different feelings one is left with are a clue to their respective particular and personal dilemmas – the struggles or challenges that they are facing. Whenever one works with people there will be some emotional work to be done, and part of this work involves attempting to come to terms with, understand, and digest the feelings evoked. In other words, the emotional work will involve a role or function as a container, processing what is felt to be unmanageable or unbearable to another. Part of one's role may be to return the feelings to the other in a more manageable form, through a comment that conveys understanding of what it is that they are experiencing.

There may, however, also be times when it is important to hold the understanding that one has and to act on the basis of the understanding rather than to return the digested feelings. This is a fundamental point. If the feelings have been unbearable, this means that the person has not been able to cope with them. The person may therefore not yet be ready to hear or think about something. It may take some time for the person to become ready. One may therefore need to contain and hold the feelings and thoughts for a while, until the person is ready to take them back. This requires patience and understanding. Should one try too early to return a feeling to someone, it is likely that their response will indicate that they are struggling. They are not likely to show a sense of being understood. Comments that make a person feel understood are more likely to help the person talk further about the things with which they have been struggling. This was the case with Tsepho. On both occasions that Anant made understanding and containing comments, this helped Tsepho to talk more about what was troubling him.

When feelings are hard to understand

Sometimes we may find that the feelings we are containing feel unmanageable. Those who work with people in distress often feel a high degree of distress themselves. This is because the emotional work of helping others think through difficult feelings requires surviving or bearing with that which feels unbearable. It is often necessary to survive the feeling of not being able to understand what the person has communicated for an extended period. Many people have commented that what they found helpful about counselling was not only the final answers that they came to, but the fact that someone accompanied them along a journey that was difficult and rather than imposing answers, helped them to find their own.

Part of what Anant did was to survive the feelings. He struggled with them for some time before he was able to make sense of them. The fact that a feeling takes a long time to understand is important information in and of itself. It is a clue to how distressing, disturbing, or difficult to comprehend the feeling is for the other person. After all, if the feeling weren't unmanageable in the first place, the person would most likely be able to manage it by themselves!

Feelings evoked by your organization

Feelings that we have in the context of our place of work do not only relate to communications from others and to our own issues. Feelings can also be evoked by the challenges that an organization is facing itself. Many organizations in South Africa are currently undergoing massive change. Because the context in which organizations are operating is changing so rapidly, many people's understanding of their organization's role has been thrown into question. People are asking themselves how best they can and should adjust to the changing demands placed on them by government, funding agencies, and the market place. These changing requirements place many demands on organizations to reposition themselves to fit their new contexts. The changes have lead to a whole range of emotional responses by people working within these organizations. The feelings that are evoked in staff are likely to contain useful information about the nature of the challenges the organization is facing, as well as the ways in which staff are responding to the changes. The emotional experience of staff (including stress, demotivation and so on) should not, therefore, simply be regarded by organizations as a problem they need to rid themselves of. Rather, it is something that needs to be understood. A central task of managers should be to understand and work with (in other words, contain) the feelings that staff members are having. This will provide staff with a greater ability to think about the challenges they are facing. Refer to Chapter 7 for a fuller discussion of the implications of these ideas for organizations.

Containment and the pressure to put things right

Taking time to understand is not always easy. Often we feel pressured to put the situation right immediately; a teacher feels pressure to help a child learn, a counsellor feels pressure to solve a person's problem, or a manager feels pressure to resolve a dispute. Part of the emotional work that is required is about letting go of this pressure, and realizing that emotional work sometimes takes time. Importantly, the feeling of pressure to solve something might itself be part of the emotional communication. A feeling of desperation may be part of what the other person has communicated and may be part of what one needs to hold. The person may be feeling that if things are not solved now, there will be a catastrophe. Apart from crisis situations (which do require prompt action) it is unlikely that such dire consequences will follow.

Do I give advice?

Clients often ask counsellors what it is that they should do. Counsellors often feel that they should give their clients some answer or advice. In these situations, the client will have communicated a sense of feeling desperate – that they don't know what to do and that their situation and their feelings are unmanageable. Until the person is able to think about and process things to some degree by themselves they are likely to continue acting in the way they have before, in other words they may not yet be ready to hear advice.

In some instances, however, it may be helpful to give a client a firm suggestion. Sometimes your holding and processing a thought is not all that a person requires. In certain circumstances a firmer response may be needed. Similarly, there may be times when a person needs to be confronted with the reality of the consequences of their actions. Sometimes people need a sense that there is an authority who knows what needs to be done. This is similar to the feeling of assurance that a child has when he or she thinks that their parent knows what to do and will protect them. If a person is feeling insecure, part of what they may need is a sense that there is someone who can give them firm guidance and who can take authority in a situation. In certain instances, counsellors who respond in this way to their clients may, therefore, be responding to a need that has been communicated by the other, just as a mother acts in a calming way to her hungry baby.

Acting when you can't contain

We need to think carefully about when it is that we step into action, particularly if our desire to take action stems from the fact that we find that the feelings that have been evoked in us are unbearable. When the feelings evoked in us are unmanageable we may cease to be able to listen. In a sense, we stop being able to contain. It as though we close our minds to the communications of others. At these times we may find ourselves wishing to take a leap into action, hoping that by acting we will take away the feelings. Sometimes counsellors who are controlling or authoritarian may respond in this way because the feelings that have been communicated to them are unmanageable or incomprehensible. To the person who is seeking help, this will be felt as rejection, in the same way that a baby who cries and whose mother is unable to understand the cry feels rejected. The feeling of not being listened to is painful and one may feel like one is being actively rejected. If this were to occur regularly to a baby, he or she might later tend to have difficulties in thinking about feelings, or might find particular kinds of feelings hard to cope with. In a similar way, if we are unable to listen to certain kinds of feelings, we will be unable to help others with these feelings.

A difficult task

This may seem to present a dilemma. When is the right time to offer an understanding? When does someone need to be confronted with something? Does someone need firm advice, or a listening ear? How does one find the answers to these questions? These may at times feel like unmanageable decisions. Understanding the meaning of the feelings one is having, attempting to process them, or initially just surviving them, may require finding a container of one's own to help one think about the feelings. We may need the help of another to think through our responses. Anant, for example, battled on his own at first, and then talked his meeting with Tsepho through with a colleague. His colleague's comment that the doctor might also have been struggling to deal with a difficult patient helped him to think about how he had been thrown by the meeting and how hard things must have been for Tsepho. By seeking the containing mind of his colleague, who returned to him a thought-through response, Anant was able to think for himself about the difficulties Tsepho had brought to him.

Blind spots

Working with people who are troubled evokes many powerful feelings. It is very difficult to manage these feelings if they relate to our own difficulties or unresolved issues. Helping someone with loss while we ourselves are coming to terms with a loss is an example. We might find it too much to think about or contain the pain that the other person is experiencing if it reminds us too intensely of our own pain. This can lead to a situation in which we are unable to think about the other person's feelings in a way that is helpful to them. We have a blind spot, so to speak.

Another example of a blind spot is when we find it difficult to allow people to be angry with us. This would mean that if a person needed to be angry with us, or was legitimately angry with us, we would find it hard to think about this, and might act in order to stop the person being angry. This is important, because sometimes we have to acknowledge that for somebody else we may seem to be something that we do not wish to be. An abused child, for example, may have come to be very untrusting of adults (for the very good reason that in his or her experience adults are untrustworthy). In his or her mind we may seem to be a potential abuser. If we cannot allow ourselves to entertain the possibility that another could see us in this way, we will not be able to help them. We will not be able to hold and contain the thought that in another's experience we are dangerous and potentially hurtful. We would thus find it hard to understand and contain the complicated and powerful feelings that are evoked when working with a child who has been abused.

It may not feel safe to discuss one's personal feelings with colleagues or supervisors. If our work is touching our personal issues, however, it is very important that these issues be attended to. This may involve seeking out someone who is able to help us understand these feelings. Consider the example of Anant once more. Many of the feelings evoked in him by the meeting

Scapegoating: a form of containing anxiety that leads to discrimination

One of the most painful aspects about the way in which people have responded to the HIV/AIDS epidemic is that various groups have come to be scapegoats for the disease. A scapegoat was originally a goat upon which the sins of a community were cast. When the goat was slaughtered, the sins were cleansed and the community freed of its collective burden. In a sense, the goat functioned as a container to hold the anxieties felt by the community. Many groups, particularly black people, women, and homosexuals, have become scapegoats for fears about HIV/AIDS. In other words, the fears we have regarding HIV/AIDS are projected onto these groups, thereby freeing us of them but burdening the scapegoats. This process is about finding someone to blame.

Another way of describing scapegoats is to say that they have been *stigmatized*. Stigma has at least four characteristics:

- Firstly, the problem that is stigmatized needs to be locatable, away from those doing the stigmatizing. In other words, it needs to be controllable.
- Secondly, the stigmatized person or group needs to be identifiable. (Often certain signs, called stigmata, are found which are then regarded as markers of the stigma. Thinness is one such stigma that marks HIV/AIDS.)
- Thirdly, the stigma must in some way be associated with the stigmatized person or group.
- Finally, the stigmatized are related to in a way that disempowers, excludes, and controls them – by extension the problem is then also controlled.

We saw that one of Tsepho's main difficulties was coping with the stigma of being HIV positive. He experienced rejection because people felt that he was a threat to them. Despite the fact that HIV cannot be contracted by casual contact, people still exclude and isolate those who have been diagnosed as HIV positive.

Why does scapegoating occur? Some authors have argued that HIV/AIDS evokes anxieties about sexuality, vulnerability to illness, and more fundamentally, vulnerability to chaos, loss of control, and ultimately annihilation and death (Gilman, 1988). In order to be protected from these fears, scapegoats are found. In other words, people are unable to manage the anxieties that HIV evokes and seek a container in which to place them. It is usually the socially marginalized or disempowered that become stigmatized because they often tend to fit the four characteristics described above. These people are often already discriminated against and isolated. Carrying the HIV/AIDS stigma further exacerbates the discrimination they face.

had a direct link with what Tsepho had communicated to him. Some feelings related to Anant's own life. It would seem that Anant's feeling of disappointment in Doctor Lin relates to a need that he has to see her in a particular way. What was important was that Anant was able to keep his own feelings and those that related to Tsepho separate. This can sometimes be a difficult task, and requires that we pay close attention to the feelings that have been evoked in us.

Of course, our responses to someone else are always going to be based on our own personalities, and in this way all our responses will be personal ones. The questions that need to be asked, in order to begin to differentiate personal feelings from feelings evoked by communication, include, "Why did this touch me in this way, and why now?" and "Another person may not have touched me in this way. What does the fact that this has touched me in this way tell me about what is being communicated to me?"

Providing containment: some key points to remember

- When feelings are overwhelming or very painful, we need someone else who can understand our feelings in order to help us to cope. In other words, we need a container to hold and understand our feelings.
- A container is someone who takes on our feelings, comes to understand them, and holds them until we are ready to understand them. Remember the jug metaphor – when the jug that holds our feelings overflows, we need another jug to store our feelings until we are ready to take them back. A container doesn't just store feelings though, a container works to understand the feelings too. So when we get our feelings back, some sense has been made of them and this helps us to understand and cope.
- Whenever we work with people, emotions will be evoked in us. If we wish to provide containment to others, we need to work to understand the feelings that are evoked in us when we work with people.
- Understanding our own feelings is the starting point for understanding the feelings of others. Unless we know ourselves we will find it hard to understand others.
- The feelings that will be evoked in us when working with people are of two kinds – those that relate to ourselves and those that we have been asked to contain by another person.
- The feelings we have when working with people are valuable clues to the issues that people are struggling with.

- Understanding feelings can take time. We need to have patience with others and ourselves. We need to remember that sometimes we will not understand immediately. Sometimes what is needed is to tolerate and survive the difficult feeling of not understanding. This is not easy, but is an essential part of the process of helping others cope with feelings.
- At times, helping others cope with feelings will feel too much. We may feel like we do not know what to do or say. This is because helping others may stir up our own issues or blind spots. At other times we may find that we are unable to understand the feelings of another. In these times, we will need to find someone who can help us understand and cope. In other words, we will need to find a container of our own. This may be a therapist, a counsellor, or someone else we can confide in to help us with our own feelings, or a supervisor or colleague to help us with our client's feelings.

CHAPTER 4

The past in the present

Our past experiences influence our lives in the present. Understanding how the past influences the present enables us to see meaning in behaviour or feelings that at first seem confusing. If we know the reasons why we do things, we have more freedom to make other choices.

As counsellors we need to understand the roots of people's beliefs about themselves. For everyone, our basic beliefs about ourselves and others are linked to experiences during our formative years. Experiences with others leave us with assumptions about how people relate to us and about how people relate to one another. Let's consider the ways in which people's behaviour and feelings develop.

Developing a sense of trust and security

If we have had good experiences – in which our basic needs have been adequately met and in which we have been effective and instrumental in getting them met – we experience the world as a benign place and we will feel that we are able to be effective in it. We will have a sense that we are able to trust others and ourselves. If we have experienced frustration and survived it, and afterwards have still been able to have our needs met, we will be more able to tolerate pain and frustration in the future.

These sorts of experiences help build our fundamental and basic beliefs about ourselves. These beliefs and assumptions include a sense of our capacity to be effective in the world as well as our sense of the predictability and reliability of others. In short, if our experiences with primary caregivers have been good enough, we develop a basic trust in ourselves. We also develop a sense of trust in the capacity of others to look after themselves. We develop a basic sense of confidence and self-esteem.

It is important to note that our experiences need to be *good enough*, not necessarily perfect. In fact, being able to survive frustration is important in developing a capacity to tolerate ambiguity, failure, frustration, and pain – all of which are inevitable in life.

The development of these capacities involves, in part, us having experienced the support of others who were able to contain the feelings and thoughts that we could not manage by ourselves (we talked about containment in some detail in Chapter 3). We need to have had experiences of others being able to soothe and help us to manage feelings that are unmanageable. If we have not had these sorts of experiences when young, we will tend to find it hard to soothe ourselves later in life.

The development of low self-esteem

If we have had negative experiences, of deprivation or trauma for example, our sense of our ability to trust others and ourselves may be distorted. We may trust too easily, or find it hard to trust at all. An early negative experience with someone can set up an expectation that others will respond to us in the same way in the future – that we will again be misunderstood, disappointed and so on. If we were previously abandoned, we may have an expectation that those whom we need now will also abandon us. If we have not experienced the support of someone who could hold and manage what we could not, then we will not have developed that capacity in ourselves – we will neither have learned that it is possible to contain ourselves, nor will we have learned how to contain ourselves. This may leave us with the expectation that others cannot contain our unmanageable feelings.

If we grew up with these kinds of experiences we would in all likelihood have found some way of trying to cope with them. The coping mechanisms that we employ in order to manage our experiences form another important dimension of the development of our basic assumptions or principles. These coping mechanisms include internal mental processes as well as behaviours. We tend to use these methods of coping again and again because they have proven adaptive in helping us to cope with pain or anxiety. We may hold onto them long after their usefulness is gone. Our past then comes to infuse our present because we expect the people in our life now to relate to us as those in the past did.

The ways in which we coped with our past experiences also set up patterns for coping and responding now. If, for example, we tried hard to be the good son or daughter when we were young in order to get affection or to stave off disapproval, we may now try to be the good lover, partner, or parent. We may feel that we have to fulfil others' expectations of us at the expense of our own wishes. We may tell ourselves that we must not get our hopes up, because we'll just get hurt again. We may tell ourselves that we are not good enough unless we are perfect. We may tell ourselves not to try, because then we cannot fail.

Our assumptions and our ways of coping will in the end lead us to act in certain kinds of ways. This can lead to something of a self-fulfilling prophecy. For example, if we have found that we get hurt when we place trust in another, we may, as a means of coping, strive to not be reliant on anyone. The problem with this strategy is that we never come to learn what might have happened had we taken the risk to trust someone. Also, if we approach people as though we can't trust them, we don't allow them to be trustworthy. We may push them to feel and act in a particular way (although clearly this depends on a person having a tendency to respond in this way). A vicious circle is created. Problems that we experience in relationships may then result from the fact that we relate to others in terms of assumptions, which in turn are based on our prior experiences. While our assumptions may be based on real experiences and may have been adaptive at one point, they may no longer be valid.

Amien and Candice

These assumptions and ways of coping are likely to repeat themselves in our interactions with others, and sometimes, the feelings that we have when we work with people are related to these sorts of processes. These ideas are perhaps best understood through reflection on examples drawn from the actual lives of people. The following example concerns the interaction between Candice, a human resources manager, and Amien, an employee who comes to her for advice.

Amien was working as a supervisor in the warehouse of a retail company. He took his job seriously and had high hopes for his career, but felt that he was constantly being passed over for promotion. He was very frustrated and felt that he was falling behind his peers.

Amien's struggle with feeling inferior

Amien was the eldest of three children. His parents had a poor relationship and they fought often, verbally and occasionally physically. Amien's father was a very critical man, both of his wife and his children. He never seemed to be satisfied with anything that Amien did. Amien's experiences with his father left him with a very deep doubt of his own worth. He came to be very critical of himself. In an attempt to put these feelings to one side, and to not let them affect him, he strove to be perfect. He was never satisfied unless things were perfect, but never felt that they were. This led him into times of paralysis when he would not begin a task, feeling that he would not be able to get it right. Amien would become very frustrated with himself, as well as intolerant of the mistakes or shortcomings of others.

Amien had felt like he was falling behind and not achieving for most of his life. He came to fear figures in authority, expecting them to criticize him as his father constantly had. Amien tended to hear slights and insults where none existed. It was as though he had been primed from a young age to expect insults and humiliation, rather than support and understanding. Secretly, he felt himself to be worthless. When he walked into Candice's office, he expected her to be critical of him and was on his guard from the start.

Candice's need to be helpful

Like Amien, Candice was the eldest of three children. Her mother was prone to depression and Candice often found herself playing the role of her mother's confidant. Her father found his wife's depressed feelings hard to bear and he often withdrew from her. Candice came to play a supportive role to her mother. She worried about her mother a lot and often felt very angry with her father. At the same time, she felt sorry for him, sensing that he couldn't cope with painful things.

Like Amien, Candice tended to try to get everything perfect, and tended to be self-critical and self-doubting. She had, however, found a great deal of esteem in being able to help her mother. Listening to her mother had made her feel needed and valued and she tried hard to convince her mother that things would be all right. At times though she felt angry with her mother. Sometimes her mother did not want to talk to her, or would not do what she suggested. At other times she felt angry when she needed something from her mother and it seemed that her mother was not aware of what she needed.

Amien and Candice's conversation

Amien and Candice had chatted in the cafeteria a couple of times. Amien felt that he could trust Candice, so he called her up and made an appointment. He felt anxious when he went to see her.

Candice was surprised that Amien had asked to talk to her, as she had not been very friendly to him in the cafeteria. She'd thought that he was trying to chat her up and had been warned off by her friends who told her that he got defensive very easily and was difficult to get on with. "Well," Candice said rather awkwardly, "I guess we should start with why it is that you've come to see me."

Amien looked uncomfortable. "Well, uh, this is hard," he said. "Well, I'm thirty-three. I've been here over five years. Guys who have been here two years have been promoted over me. I'm good at what I do. I get on with the job." As he spoke, Amien did not make eye contact with Candice. "When I deal with questions from the branches, I'm straight with them. I'm starting to think someone in management just doesn't like me. I'm getting angry." After a short pause, during which Candice said nothing, Amien continued, "I just like things to be precise, to be done well. Some people just aren't efficient. If I'm going to do a job, I do it well, and I expect others to do the same."

"Have you spoken with your manager?" Candice asked.

"That wouldn't help. He wouldn't understand. It's not worth it," Amien replied somewhat curtly and looking angry.

Candice felt put down. She felt like she'd said something stupid. She tried again. "Maybe if you spoke with him and explained your concerns. Who is he, uh, what's his name?"

Amien looked at Candice contemptuously and said, "I thought you would be helpful. Don't you think I've thought of that? It wouldn't help, he's got a vendetta against me."

Candice felt a little stunned and was quiet.

"I got into a fight with him because he said I was too impatient with the admin people. I told him that they have to do their jobs and that our company is getting a bad name because people don't follow through on what they promise."

"Did you get angry with the admin people?" Candice asked.

"Yes! And I'm bloody glad I did. At least they did what they were supposed to."

Candice felt like pointing out to Amien that had he handled the situation more calmly, he might not have such a poor relationship with his manager. She was too nervous to actually say this to him though and felt annoyed with Amien. She felt like she just wasn't getting through to him. "Maybe your manager is just trying to look after the admin staff," she suggested.

"But what about them having to do their jobs properly?" Amien asked sarcastically.

Candice again felt like she'd been told off and felt even more angry and frustrated. "Maybe, but sometimes people do things if we talk nicely to them."

Amien suddenly looked very hurt. "Are you saying that there's something wrong with how I talk to people?"

Candice felt that there was something wrong, but to say so to Amien would provoke something. "Maybe," she ventured cautiously.

Amien looked even more hurt and tears welled up in his eyes. "I don't think so. They just need a kick up the pants. I've got to go, I'm late for an appointment." He left the room in a rush.

Candice was left feeling angry with Amien, but she somehow felt sorry for him. As he left the room she thought to herself that he looked like a little sulking boy. The interaction left Candice with powerful feelings. Amien had made her feel that everything she suggested was wrong. He made her feel stupid and put down. Thinking about it afterwards, she felt that this was unfair of him because there was nothing wrong with what she had suggested. She thought to herself that although it might be difficult for him to acknowledge, it was likely that Amien had played a part in alienating his colleagues. After all, she had tried to be helpful to him and this had angered him. It seemed to her that Amien did not want to hear anything objective. Candice agreed with her friends who found Amien to be defensive. She felt that her efforts to understand him had been misunderstood. Candice felt angry and frustrated.

What can we understand about Candice and Amien's interaction?

Imagine that we are in Candice's position and our job is to help Amien. How would we begin to understand the meaning of the way in which he responded? Candice's reactions to Amien contain the seeds for understanding the meaning of Amien's way of relating.

There are several important things to take note of in Candice's response. Firstly, she felt put down and stupid. Secondly, she felt that Amien wouldn't listen objectively to her. (Thinking about it later though, Candice realized that what she said to Amien was not stupid.) Thirdly, Candice felt oddly sorry for him as Amien left the room. Lastly, Candice felt angry and frustrated because she was not able to get through to him.

For his part, Amien felt inferior and put down, in much the same way that Candice came to feel. As we have seen, Amien tends to expect that others will be critical of him in the same way that he is critical of himself. He expects that others will see through him and will reject him. Candice's comments about him having been part of the problem felt threatening as they made him feel that he was being found out and he felt humiliated. Amien's past has led him to expect criticism. Amien had gone to Candice hoping to find someone who would side with him. He felt alone and that people did not take the time to understand him. He felt angry with Candice because he felt that she had minimized what he had had to say. He also felt that she had blamed him for what was going wrong. As the tears had welled up in his eyes, he had felt very alone and weak, just like he had as a boy listening to his father's criticisms of him. As a boy, he had begun to tell himself to pull himself together, telling himself that it was useless and weak to feel like this. Nevertheless, he was very much like a small scared boy as he left Candice's office.

Hearing someone point out that his own behaviour contributed to his problems made Amien feel criticized. His dilemma was that if he acknowledged his part in things then he would feel guilty and inferior. Amien has felt alone and misunderstood for most of his life. Having someone point out his part in making things not work for himself would confront him with this fact. He appears to struggle with the feeling of being wrong.

Candice got angry because her attempts at helping him were turned down. This rebuff challenged her basic assumption that she is needed and worthwhile if she is helpful. It made her feel unneeded.

Amien expected a certain kind of response from Candice. He expected to be criticized. When Candice tried to talk to him about his part in his difficulties, he felt criticized. What we know of his background tells us that this expectation of criticism is linked to his experiences with his father, which led him to assume that people in authority would criticize him. His relationship with his father had also left him with a deep doubt about himself. Part of the reason that he felt as hurt as he did about Candice's response was that it echoed the hurt he felt when his father used to criticize him. He left her office feeling like a scolded boy. In many ways, Amien related to Candice as though she were the same kind of critical figure as his father. This process, whereby someone relates to another in the same way as to a significant figure from his or her past, is described by the term *transference*.

Transference

The term transference refers to a process that occurs when feelings related to a significant person (often, but not always, a significant figure from one's past) are *transferred* to another relationship. One begins to feel and act as though the person to whom one's feelings are transferred will act in a similar way to significant figures in the past. It seems that Amien has transferred some of his feelings about his father to Candice. We would describe this by saying that his transference to Candice involved feelings of inferiority, anger, and an expectation of criticism.

In psychotherapy the notion of transference is used principally to refer to a situation where feelings that a person has for another are transferred to a therapist. Transference goes further than this though: the person also relates to the therapist in terms of his or her past feelings and relationships and interprets what the therapist does and says in terms of the past. In many ways, this is what Amien was doing with Candice's words. He interpreted them through the lens provided by his past relationship with his father and the ways in which he coped with that relationship. Furthermore, his characteristic way of always expecting criticism (also based on his past) was also played out with Candice.

In psychotherapy a great deal of healing occurs through being able to come to understand what we expect and assume of our therapist and how this is related to feelings associated with significant figures in our lives. Coming to understand these expectations and assumptions often involves confronting a lot of difficult feelings about our experiences, feelings that we may have been attempting to put to one side. If we experience these feelings and come to understand how our past experiences have affected how we see others and ourselves now, we can be free to make choices that were previously unavailable to us. We gain perspective on how our relationships with important people in our past have affected how we see others and ourselves. Through talking about our needs and expectations of the therapist, we come to renegotiate the terms of our relationship with the therapist. Our assumptions about how the relationship was going to work are unpacked and we learn to understand a set of new terms and assumptions about ourselves and others, which can then be applied in other relationships.

Transference in other settings

The process of transference is part of everyday life. People see their experiences in terms of the lenses they have acquired while growing up and talk about 'emotional baggage'. However, not all the meaning that people attach to experience is necessarily related to past authority figures, such as parents. Meaning is also related to a person's hopes and wishes. Their cultural, religious, and political values also play a role. In South Africa, racial issues carry particular meaning. Racism, and worries about whether other people are racist, often come up in situations where people of different races work and meet together. Because of the history of the artificial separation of people classified as belonging to different races, it is well worth bearing these factors in mind when seeking to understand the meanings people ascribe to race and how they affect their interactions with others. This is also important because many people in South Africa have experienced trauma as a result of their race. Race may thus carry a specific meaning for some that is associated with having been hurt.

Unresolved feelings that we have not yet come to understand and contain for ourselves are often stirred up when we are under stress. Consequently, in a situation of stress, transference may occur. Transference is also likely to occur where there are relationships involving differences in power and authority, or where there is a need for one person to depend on another. These aspects of relationships are likely to evoke feelings related to similar needs or relationships in the past. As the example of Candice and Amien shows, transference often occurs in the work context. It is likely that during interviews, performance appraisals, disciplinary hearings and so on, where anxieties are heightened, people's coping mechanisms and assumptions are elicited and a transference of these to colleagues may occur.

Transference is also likely to occur between children and their teachers. Teachers play an important part in children's lives, and the bonds between children and teachers become strong. Because of the amount of time teachers and pupils spend together, as well as the need for teachers to discipline children and the fact that learning evokes anxiety for many children, a transference of feelings to teachers is very common. Children are also likely to find safety and security in teachers who often come to play an important stabilizing role in children's lives.

Winston: a boy who cannot trust

Ten-year-old Winston ran away from home because his father regularly came home drunk and beat him, his mother, and his two brothers. Winston felt that he couldn't

take it any more – he was so angry and felt very desperate. On the street some older boys let him join their group, but they were mean to him, ordering him around and beating him up. He then went to a centre for street children and the care-worker there took him to a similar shelter closer to his home. A social worker put him in touch with his family and he would go home some weekends, but during the week he slept at the shelter. At school Winston could hardly concentrate. A good part of his school day was spent either sleeping or staring out the classroom window. Winston bullied the other children and started to smoke marijuana. When a male teacher tried to discipline him, Winston became furious. Teachers began to ignore him – with more than forty children in the class it was hard to give attention to one troublesome boy who didn't seem to want help. Winston started to feel that he didn't care about himself or his future.

What would Winston's transference be to this male teacher? Why did he get angry with the teacher and why does it seem that he doesn't want help? Winston's expectation of males in authority is that they are threatening figures. It is very likely that Winston would not believe that the teacher actually cared for him and was concerned for him. It is also likely that the anger he felt when the teacher disciplined him was related to the fact that he had been presented with care and attention but believed that he was unable to rely on it.

Transference is also highly likely in medical and emergency services settings, where people may have strong feelings evoked by the stress of being ill or in crisis. In these situations, medical or emergency personnel are not only called upon to fulfil a technical, medical, or rescue function, but are also often required to contain high levels of emotional distress. Medical and emergency personnel have a myriad of demands made of them, many of which involve transference. In other words, part of the way in which people understand their illnesses and trauma depends on their past experiences. Their relationships with their caregiving personnel will replay their relationships with caregivers in the past. Not only do caregiving personnel need to manage their clients' feelings, but also their own responses to the trauma or illness with which they are working.

Counter-transference

The term *counter-transference* refers to feelings evoked in counsellors or therapists during their work with clients. Counter-transference feelings include feelings that relate to one's own issues, as well as those evoked by the client. Thus, for example, the feelings that are evoked in a paramedic by an injured motorist will involve his or her own response to treating an injured person, as well as the feelings that the motorist is asking him or her to contain. The injured person may be very frightened and part of the paramedic's job is to calm him or her and contain his or her anxieties.

Winston: the counter-transference he evokes

Part of Winston's teachers' counter-transference was to feel helpless with regard to his intransigence, a kind of giving up. This is similar to what Winston is feeling. His inability to trust and his consequent angry response to the teacher led the staff at the school to give up on him. It is as though they have said to him, "Okay, have it your way." This illustrates how one's transference can push another into feeling something. Winston has no one to help him understand his feelings. It is tragic that the pressures on the staff at school have made it hard for them to understand Winston's feeling. If they were to reflect on their own feelings of helplessness they might gain some insight into what Winston is feeling.

Working with one's counter-transference

A central task of all those who work with people is to develop knowledge and insight into their own feelings in order to differentiate between feelings that are related to their own pasts, and feelings that they are asked to contain for others. Perhaps the most important task, however, is to understand the relation between these two sorts of feelings. This understanding of what our feelings mean is what is involved in containing them (discussed in detail in Chapter 3). The goal is to not become overwhelmed by these feelings, or to act impulsively on them. We must rather attempt to understand why we might be feeling them. When we have strong feelings evoked by another, we need to ask ourselves, "Is this something about me, or is it something about the other person?" Winston's teachers could have asked questions like, "Why are we feeling helpless about this boy? Maybe we feel like this because we are overworked and there are so many boys like him? Maybe our feelings can tell us something about how he is feeling?"

Being comfortable with not knowing

Asking these sorts of questions is not easy. Taking the step to look at what we are feeling is hard, particularly when we are under pressure. Strong feelings may make us feel confused. They may make us feel like we do not know what to do. It is important to remember that an understanding of what someone else is feeling is something that one strives for. It is the nature of work with feelings that we will often not understand someone completely. Often we will not understand at all. We need to remind ourselves that coming to understand feelings improves with time. We also need to accept, however, that every time we work with someone there will be times when we don't understand the meaning of his or her feelings. It is important to recognize that not knowing is part of the process of coming to contain and understand feelings. If the feelings were understandable, the person would in all likelihood have managed them by themselves in the first place. The fact that the feelings are difficult is why they have asked for help and we need to feel comfortable with the fact that understanding them will take time.

Let us consider the example of Candice and Amien once more. At the end of their talk, Candice is only able to know what Amien's issues are at a certain level. She has some sense of what his difficulties are but she does not have the history that we do. What she does know, however, is enough of a starting point to help her to decide where to go from here. She has important clues to help her begin to decide how best to help him.

It is very uncomfortable to not understand. However, being able to survive the feeling of not knowing is one of the key tasks of a counsellor. One of the most useful ways of coming to understand our counter-transference is to be able to talk it though with another person, to find our own container for these feelings.

Blind spots

As we discussed in the chapter on containment, we may find that we have certain blind spots. In other words, we may find certain feelings difficult to cope with. These blind spots, which we all have, relate to feelings that we ourselves have not yet resolved. Some of us may have difficulty discussing certain kinds of feelings, such as those that pertain to anger or sexuality. These blind spots make it hard for us to think freely about the other person's feelings. Candice, for example, felt that because Amien did not seem to want her help she was not needed. This angered her because it reminded her of how she felt when she was a child and her help was refused by her mother.

We all have certain kinds of issues and feelings that we find harder to cope with than others. It is very worth our while to become familiar with these.

The more we learn about them, the more forgiving we can become of ourselves. Often the things we have the most difficulty with will stir up the most feelings. It is very important to try to find someone who can help us think through these feelings (for example by chatting with someone we trust, like a supervisor). Coming to understand our blind spots can be a very important part of our personal growth.

Working with transference

It should be clear that transference occurs in many settings, but how do we work with it? An important distinction may be drawn between managing transference and interpreting transference. *Managing* transference involves being aware of the transference and how it affects our own feelings and those of others, and then acting in accordance with the understanding. *Interpreting* transference involves discussing the link between feelings for someone in the present and feelings for a figure in the past. Whether we manage or interpret transference, or do both, depends on the nature of our work.

If our task is counselling, for example, then it is important to try to understand what a client is expecting of us and what they need. In counselling situations transference will always be a factor, but it may not be necessary or desirable to interpret it. Making a comment about the link between the feelings a client has for you as his or her therapist and their root in the past may feel very threatening to a patient. Likewise, a teacher does not need to make explicit to his or her pupils the link between the children's feelings for the teacher and their feelings for their parents. When they are made, such comments should in any event be made tentatively, for they are hypotheses and we need to be prepared to discard or modify our ideas if we realize we have misunderstood. Candice, for example, was correct in commenting to Amien that his way of relating to others was part of the problem, but her timing was inappropriate. He was not ready to hear her. Because his inability to trust people was an issue that had not been clarified between them, her comments did not serve to build a sense of trust with him. What she said to him was consequently felt as critical and attacking.

Managing the transference

Managing the transference involves making decisions to act in certain ways and being mindful of the implications for the other person of these actions.

The first step in managing the transference is to contain the unmanageable feelings that the other has. If we are to help someone who fears that we may disappoint them, we must be able to hold in our minds the understanding that the person is frightened and that what we need to do is to act in accordance with this, taking care that our actions do not hurt them even more. We need to ask questions such as the following, "Will what we do reinforce their assumptions?" "Do we want to do that?" "Is it unavoidable that we will reinforce their assumptions?" "What are the implications of doing this?" "Are there steps we need to put in place to change the message we are giving?" "Does the person need to hear another message, one that might be different to messages they have heard before?"

Managing transference requires that we take on a degree of responsibility because it involves recognizing the implications of our actions for another's sense of himself or herself. This is also why it is important to adhere to the boundaries that we establish in setting up a counselling relationship, like maintaining confidentiality for example.

The function of clear limits and consequences for behaviour in schools or other places where work involves people in need is in part to manage the transference. When working with children in need, whose transference to their caregivers is likely to involve worries about whether it is safe to trust their caregivers, being consistent and reliable is very important. It gives the message that one is dependable and thus trustworthy. For a child like Winston, whom we met earlier in the chapter, the setting of these sorts of boundaries and the provision of consistency and reliability would be very important in helping him to develop a sense that figures in authority can be dependable and trustworthy. It is likely that doing this will provoke a period of testing, as Winston and children who have had similar experiences will not easily believe in the trustworthiness of authority figures. Also, the presence of consistent limits and care is likely to provoke a lot of pain in Winston, as it will confront him with the sorts of things he has missed out on. It is very likely that a considerable amount of transference anger will be evoked, as the teacher who tried to discipline him discovered. Part of the job of managing this kind of transference is to help the child find appropriate ways of expressing his anger.

While it is important that consistency, reliability and so on be maintained, the fact remains that sometimes we will disappoint people. When this happens, it's important to not pretend that it didn't happen, perhaps out of a fear of feeling that we have failed. It is much more worthwhile to acknowledge that a person has been disappointed and to try to come to understand the meaning that the disappointment has for that person. Helping people with their feelings in the here and now will help them with their feelings about important people in their pasts. Understanding how to respond to someone (managing the transference) thus involves understanding our own feelings first (managing our counter-transference).

Interpreting the transference

Interpretation of transference is something that happens in everyday life to some extent, such as when people talk to each other about their expectations of, or disappointments in, each other. As we have seen above, it is a key site of change in psychotherapy because it allows people to gain perspective on the ways in which they have come to assume that relationships function.

Managing the transference is often the first step in working with the transference. Knowing the meaning of feelings at a deeper or more complex level in a way that enables us to interpret the transference is an advanced skill. Also, knowing the meaning of feelings in this way develops over time as a relationship progresses. It is only with time that we can come to understand the full implications and meaning of a client's feelings. However, an examination of how we are feeling in and after interactions is often enough to help us to begin to decide where to go with things.

In most situations it is usually not necessary to interpret the transference. More often than not, it is sufficient to act with an understanding of the transference implications of our actions (in other words, to manage the transference). In certain instances, however, helping people to understand the assumptions they are making and the meanings of the feelings they are having, is important. This is because for some people the nature of the assumption is difficult to challenge simply on the basis of actions. If, for example, a person is operating with the assumption that others are not trustworthy, even actions that seem to indicate that another is trustworthy can be discounted as invalid evidence. Having been disappointed before, the person might have decided not to get his or her hopes up. By holding onto the assumption that people are untrustworthy, the person feels safer – they attempt to insulate themselves against the pain of being disappointed again. In order to shift this sort of assumption, its roots need to be understood. Making a link for someone between the fact that they got hurt in the past, and are now shielding themselves from others to avoid getting hurt again, may help them to understand how what they feel and believe affects their lives in the present.

Coping mechanisms and transference

Transference involves people's usual ways of coping with pain becoming reactivated. If they are worried, for example, about being hurt again by you (the therapist), then they will attempt to cope with their feelings for you in the same way that they have always coped with them. This raises the very important issue of why it is that people maintain these assumptions.

The transference implications of working with traumatized people

One of the most powerful effects of trauma is that it fundamentally alters a person's basic sense of the predictability of the world. As a result, a person's sense of trust is usually also affected. Traumatized people might find it very hard to trust and feel secure after their experience, or they might become overly trusting, placing trust too easily and too quickly. It is as though trauma disrupts the process of understanding who is trustworthy and why. Issues of trust and security are therefore often central in work with traumatized people and become so, ironically enough, at the very time of their heightened need for someone to care for them, to understand them, and for them to make sense of the traumatic event. Because of this, the emotional work that is necessary – the processing of what we need to contain – is often immense. We need to contain very powerful feelings of anger, guilt, shame and so on. We need to contain the thought that we may be a potential abuser in the eyes of the client.

When working with traumatized people powerful feelings related to our own losses and trauma may be evoked. It is important that we are able to understand this – we will often need support of our own in order to do so, and supervision to think through the processes involved.

The feelings evoked by childhood sexual abuse often leave the survivors feeling very unsure of themselves. Those survivors who did not have someone to help them make sense of their experience and were left to their own devices, often do not know whether what they feel is valid. In a sense they lacked the container that would help them to come to terms with the experience of being abused. Thus, in the transference there may be worries on the survivor's part about whether or not the counsellor will be someone who will understand. Negotiating issues of trust and reliability will be paramount. For these reasons, adhering to the contracts that have been drawn up will be of vital importance.

Working with transference and counter-transference: some advice

- One of the single most useful sources of information for understanding the emotional meaning of interactions is your own emotional response, your counter-transference.
- Coming to understand your counter-transference will help you to understand the transference, because it will give you insights into the kinds of feelings that the person you are helping evokes in others. This gives clues to what troubles them.
- Understanding your counter-transference involves understanding three different kinds of feelings and their interaction:
  those that you find difficult to talk about (your blind spots);
  those that are evoked in you by your work (the kinds of buttons people press in you); and
  those that you are asked to contain by your clients (the feelings you feel when you are empathically attuned to someone)
  One needs to understand the relationship between all these feelings and how they mix together.
- Allow yourself time to understand your counter-transference feelings. You cannot be expected to understand them all at once. In fact, understanding your counter-transference is something that you will be engaged in for as long as you work with people. Remember, it is part of the work to feel confused and to not understand sometimes. When we are under a lot of pressure it is often hard to do this and we feel overwhelmed. It is important to find some way of dealing with this pressure in order to get a clear head again.
- Managing the transference means that your interactions with the person are guided by an understanding of the transference. This means that understanding the transference is the first step in managing the transference.
- Ask yourself what your actions mean to the person in terms of the transference. This will guide you in understanding how they see you and what they need.
- If you let someone down, acknowledge that this has happened and work from there. It is impossible not to disappoint people at times. It is better to try to see what meaning this has for the person. Helping them through their disappointment in you may help them through their disappointment in others, which may be at the root of their transference.

- Managing the transference sometimes means accepting that in the eyes of someone else we have negative qualities. Helping them involves accepting that we are seen like that. If the way in which someone sees you troubles you, you need to understand it more, for it may be a blind spot and it may also say a lot about the things that trouble the other. Often the things that we struggle with the most will evoke the most feeling in us.
- It is very important that you talk through your feelings with another person. You need a container as well. Find a colleague you can trust or find a supervisor. If you have troubling blind spots, perhaps you need to find a therapist or counsellor as well.

Chapter 5

Understanding trauma

Trauma is widespread in society and can have serious effects not only on those exposed to it, but also those who offer help. Even organizations set up to help survivors of trauma can be badly affected unless they build in mechanisms to look after themselves.

When Chante, a very keen psychology student, was offered a volunteer position two mornings a week at the local Trauma Crisis Centre she was delighted. This would give her the opportunity she felt she had been waiting for her whole life – to help people in crisis, to learn from experienced people, and to lay the basis of a future career in trauma work.

For the first few sessions she was content to read the impressive documentation that the Trauma Crisis Centre had produced and to make use of the centre's small library and resource centre. She found staff helpful and friendly, though many of them appeared tired and frustrated in various ways. After her orientation period, Chante was allowed to go on supervised intake duty, which meant that she would take on new cases that came in, but under supervision. She was assured that she would be supported all along the way, and though she was anxious about what would happen, she was also tremendously excited. Her direct supervisor, Elana, said to her, "Always remember that in this work it's one percent training and ninety-nine percent who you are. I can see you'll be a natural. Don't worry, and don't be scared to take the plunge and take on the work."

Three weeks went by and there were no referrals on the mornings on which Chante was on duty. During the fourth week, the permanent staff went to a staff development meeting at a conference venue out of town and Chante was left to mind the telephones at the centre. She was given Elana's cellular phone number to call in the case of any emergency. Shortly after the others had left, an urgent call came in from a police officer at the station nearby. A man had been shot dead at point-blank range in front of his wife and five-year-old son, the police officer said, and the widow and child were very distraught and in urgent need of help. He was calling to say that the woman and the boy would be dropped at the Trauma Crisis Centre within the next half hour. When Chante protested that she would have to phone her supervisor, the police officer became angry.

"You're supposed to be a crisis centre," he said. "Can't you handle a crisis? They will be there soon and how you deal with this situation is your problem. I have other things to do – like trying to catch the devil that did this."

As he slammed the phone down, Chante gratefully remembered that she could call Elana, and she did so immediately, leaving an urgent message on Elana's voicemail. She then went to boil the kettle to have cup of tea ready for the distraught woman when she arrived, and for Elana, who would be sure to need it when she got back.

After ten minutes, Elana had not called back and Chante left another, more urgent, voicemail message. She felt cross with herself for not having noted down where the full-time staff were going that day, and for not having any of their numbers available. Over the next few minutes, she phoned Elana a few more times but still she reached the voicemail.

Just as she was trying to decide what to do next, a police officer arrived with a woman and a boy whom he introduced as Mrs Adams and Donovan. Thanking Chante for her help, the police officer left hastily. Chante was surprised at her own calm. She gave the woman a cup of sweet tea and then went into a back office to try to reach Elana again by phone. Then she noticed Elana's cellular phone lying on the desk. She was alone and this was a crisis. What should she do? She remembered Elana's calming words and she decided to do what she thought was best.

"Mrs Adams, Donovan, won't you come through to the office?" she said as reassuringly as she could.

"Thank you, doctor," said the woman quietly, as she and the little boy followed Chante.

Elana's office was bright and cheerful and there was a large basket of toys on the floor. Mrs Adams sat down while Donovan emptied the toys onto the floor and began to take the plastic dolls apart and throw the pieces around the room.

"So, I hear you've had a slight upset," said Chante.

Mrs Adams was silent.

"Was it a bad experience?"

More silence. Time seemed to drag on and on and eventually, remembering what she had learned about allowing clients to take their time, Chante said that this was probably not the best time for Mrs Adams to speak. Mrs Adams asked for a pill so that she and Donovan could sleep that night. Chante suggested that Mrs Adams contact her nearest community health centre about this. She gave Mrs Adams her telephone number and told her she could call her any time, day or night. She called a taxi and was surprised at both how relieved and how shaky she felt when she was on her own again.

When Elana returned to the office she was angry with Chante for having taken the case, and said she was acting beyond her field of competence. She also warned Chante that Mrs Adams would now call her day and night and there was nothing she could do about it. Chante in turn felt angry at having been left so unsupported in such difficult circumstances. She was amazed that more concern was not expressed either by Elana or by other staff for Mrs Adams and Donovan, or, indeed, for her.

Trauma is an increasingly obvious part of our society. Interpersonal violence, both public (as in war or civil unrest) and private (as in rape or child abuse within families), is of increasing concern throughout the world, and has come to the attention of all sorts of people in service positions – including health workers, educators, police, and people working in the legal system. Other forms of trauma, such as natural disasters (like tornadoes, earthquakes, and floods) and accidents (including road accidents and accidents in the home such as burns or electrocution) also take their emotional toll on individuals, families, and communities. Many psychological theories of the past – most notably Freud's – are based on an understanding of how we react and respond to trauma in our lives.

Over the past thirty years or so, people in the mental health field have tried to systematize their understanding of how people respond to trauma. According to the Fourth Edition of the *Diagnostic and Statistical Manual of the American Psychiatric Association* (1994), we can expect certain predictable responses to extreme stress. These reactions, known as *post-traumatic stress disorder* (*PTSD*), can be summarized in the following way:

- The person keeps re-experiencing the event. (For example, they have recurring nightmares, are unable to get the event out of their mind, and act or feel as if the event were happening again.)
- The person avoids situations that remind them of the trauma, or experience a general feeling of numbness. (For example, a person who was attacked on a train may now avoid train journeys; a person who before the trauma got on well with others now begins withdrawing from people.)
- The person has difficulties with what is termed 'arousal'. (For example, they have problems staying or falling asleep, are irritable and experience angry outbursts, have difficulty concentrating, are easily startled, are always on guard for danger.)

It has been estimated that about 4% of people will suffer from post-traumatic stress disorder in their lifetimes, but the risks of being exposed to trauma and violence increase markedly depending on where you live, your socio-economic status and so on. For example, a child living in a crowded home where there is no electricity for cooking is far more likely to be burned by fire than children in better socio-economic circumstances.

Where trauma is widespread and life is hard for all, communities may develop ways of dealing with trauma and life's difficulties. For example, some very poor communities will have systems whereby neighbours will offer emotional and practical assistance to people who have been bereaved, on the implicit understanding that similar help will be given to all when and if their time comes. It is also the case, though, that communities which have come to expect high levels of trauma and violence may become numb in themselves, and may lose patience with those who define themselves, or are somehow defined, as victims. Where everybody suffers, it may be expected that people should just 'get on with it'. Those who have difficulty coping may even be considered weak and deserving of punishment.

It is impossible, in any service work, not to be confronted with trauma and its effects, and this is particularly the case in violent and stressed societies. One of the key issues we need to think about in helping people cope with trauma and its effects is the social context within which the person is living. Is there a supportive or unsupportive environment? Is the person's life-situation likely to make the effects of trauma worse or better? The challenges are very different, for example, when we work with a young woman from a loving secure family who is raped by a stranger than when we work with a young woman who has been raped by her father repeatedly over many years, and who for economic reasons has very few options in terms of moving out of home.

Where abusive practices are widespread, all sorts of justifications for them may be used in communities, and these justifications can create special problems for helping individuals and organizations. For example, in some communities it is said that it is culturally acceptable for men to beat their wives. This attitude makes it especially difficult for helpers to gain community support in assisting women who have been beaten by their husbands. (In the next chapter we will learn about 'cultural camouflage' which can be used to cover not only individual abuse but also histories of abusive practices.) It is often a long historical process to change patterns of community violence, and violence prevention is easier said than done. Even encouraging community safety is challenging – one has only to think of people's objections to driving more slowly and to wearing seatbelts, both of which have been shown to reduce the risk of injury and death. Anti-smoking legislation has always been hotly opposed even though we all know that reducing smoking reduces the trauma of illness and premature death.

Trauma and our sense of the world

A common effect of a traumatic or violent experience is that it can change a person's sense of security and trust in the world and other people. When a person's home is destroyed by a flood or tornado, for example, this can lead to feelings that the whole world and all the things the person thought of doing in life, no longer have meaning – nothing will be safe and secure again. People exposed to continuous trauma or to extreme ongoing deprivation often find it very hard to plan for the future, as the future is so uncertain. This is part of why it is so hard to implement AIDS prevention programmes – or any health promotion programmes – with people who have been traumatized. If there is every chance that my life could change dramatically and unpredictably tomorrow, how meaningful can it be to me to make changes to my lifestyle that could affect my life in many years' time? The sense of life having a predictable fabric and future is interfered with.

When other people perpetrate trauma, either through carelessness or especially deliberately, this can affect our sense of trust not only in the world but also in other people. Strangers can come to be feared and mistrusted, and even previously good relationships can become poisoned and break down. A woman who has been raped by a stranger, for example, may find it difficult to continue in a relationship with a supportive male partner. It may also be in this situation, of course, that the partner himself may be struggling with the effects of the rape and may find himself drawing away from his much-loved partner who has been raped. He may even find, to his horror, that he feels at some level angry with his partner for having been raped and for having brought this trauma into the relationship. This reaction is of course neither rational nor fair, but it can be a reality that people trying to help after the rape will have to take into account.

Secondary trauma

It is clear then, that trauma affects not only the survivor of trauma but also those close to the survivor and the broader community. All the symptoms of post-traumatic stress disorder mentioned on page 66 have been found not only in trauma survivors but also in family members and in witnesses of trauma. The effects can be even more widespread. Certain professions place people at extra risk for developing PTSD. For example, military and security personnel, as well as police, are more likely than most to witness or be involved in violence. Fire fighters as well as ambulance and other emergency service personnel will in the course of their work have to deal with dead and dying people as well as mutilated bodies. Some doctors and nurses deal routinely with the results of accidents and sudden illnesses, and work on medical emergency units can be very stressful. Crime reporters and journalists who have to report on accidents, disasters, wars, and other forms of conflict may also develop PTSD symptoms. Many journalists speak of becoming emotionally numbed to the violence, crime, and misery they see – this may be part of a stress syndrome.

Counsellors and therapists who work with trauma victims may in time develop PTSD symptoms themselves. These people are said to be suffering from *vicarious* or *secondary traumatization*. There are at least two ways that this secondary traumatization can be caused. First, hearing repeatedly of traumatic events can lead one to be frightened, to question life's meaning, and to feel out of touch with other people. Second, many people who wish to help those who have been traumatized feel helpless in the face of what has happened and blocked by the responses (or lack of them) on the part of those they wish to help. Let us look again at Chante's experience and how these issues played themselves out in the Trauma Crisis Centre as an organization.

As it happens, Chante's bad experience had some very positive effects. The night of her attempt to help Mrs Adams and Donovan, she went home very shaken. To her amazement, though, Elana contacted her a few days later to apologize and also to discuss what had happened.

"I've hardly slept, Chante. I can't believe what I did to you – how I've become something I swore I would never be," she said. "I started working here three years ago, and I was incredibly excited to be doing this work and to have the opportunity to help traumatized people. I had such energy and commitment. Soon I was rushing about helping all sorts of people. I was being phoned day and night. I felt for the first time in my life that I was useful, that I was doing something that really meant something."

To Chante's amazement, Elana began to cry. She didn't know what to do, but Elana soon began to talk again. "Sorry, Chante, but don't worry about my tears – they are a good thing. You see, my whole life I wanted to help people who'd been hurt. My parents got out of Germany just before the Second World War, and all their family and friends who were left behind were killed, mostly in concentration camps. My mom especially lived with guilt her whole life for being a survivor, and for not having been able to save her own mother. As I watched this withdrawn woman whom I could never get close to, I grew more and more determined that I would make things right by helping people."

Elana paused to wipe her tears. After a while, she continued. "And here I was – working at the Trauma Crisis Centre, and helping people day and night. It was wonderful. I wished at the time that my mother could be happier with what I was doing, but she was more concerned for my safety. I found myself working harder and longer, doing more and more. Then one day I was phoned by a client who I think was a gang member who had been stabbed for the second time in a month. I shouted at him and told him it was his fault. I began to get cross with other clients, especially those who contacted me at home. I was tired of their stories – they all seemed the same, and they all seemed boring. Some of the clients seemed so stupid – not taking proper care with electricity, walking around in unsafe neighbourhoods, that kind of thing. I felt that they were asking for trouble. At home now I keep the phone off the hook – I am just too tired to be available to everyone, and I feel so bad about it. When I left my cell phone here on the day you had that difficult case, I didn't do it on purpose, but I can see now that I just wanted a day off. And also, I'm ashamed to say, Chante, I think at some level I just wanted you – the bright-eyed newcomer – to get some taste of what I have been through working here. I know you didn't mean it at all, but your enthusiasm felt to me like a slap in the face – you seemed still to be what I'd wished I could have stayed – the enthusiastic, keen helper. Here I am, after only three years, the cynical wreck, and I can't bear it. I'm so sorry."

Chante felt such a mixture of things in response to this outpouring that she didn't quite know what to say. Some of what Elana admitted to shocked her, but she could also see that Elana had great courage to be so honest. Despite Elana's admission that she had become cynical, Chante could see the part of Elana that was very caring and concerned but which had somehow got hidden under all sorts of layers of self-protection. Just as Elana could see aspects of her younger self in Chante, furthermore, Chante could strongly identify with Elana's wish to put right all sorts of things that had gone wrong in her life, and to repair some of the damage of the past. Chante wondered whether it was just coincidence, or whether there was meaning in the fact that her parents had suffered too. They had been forcibly removed from the home and community they had loved, and Chante had grown up in an impersonal small flat in a dangerous area. Her parents had never been able to make this new house a true home, and they often, though they were very young when Chante was born, described their lives as being 'over'. Chante's father drank too much and her mother said that her only pleasure in life was smoking a packet of cigarettes a day. As she thought of all these things, Chante began to wonder who were the ones in crisis and experiencing trauma – was it the clients or was it Elana and Chante?

As Elana pointed out to Chante, though, the problem went beyond the two of them – the fact was that all the staff had been prepared to leave an inexperienced student in charge when they went off, and not one of them had offered her support after her ordeal. When Elana brought this to the attention of the director of the Trauma Crisis Centre, the director arranged for a colleague from another organization to facilitate a meeting for all Trauma Crisis Centre staff, in which it emerged that almost all staff were feeling burnt out, cut off, and disappointed in the work. It emerged as well that a lot of the sick leave people had been taking had been for vague complaints – some staff came to see their sick leave as part of their attempt to get away from the horror of the work and the lack of support in the organization. It was agreed that the visiting colleague would facilitate weekly support meetings for the staff, with emphasis on self-care and care for colleagues. Part of what the staff had to learn was that looking after themselves was important for looking after their clients. They obtained some comfortable new furniture for their office, and began to take tea and lunch breaks. They helped one another set appropriate boundaries for clients, and instituted a roster scheme whereby on any one day only one person was on call after hours, so that everyone could have time off.

Holidays became compulsory! In time, and not without difficulty and uneven progress, staff seemed more able to look after clients and themselves, and to accept that there was a limited amount they could do themselves. Chante continues to work part-time as a volunteer and hopes to join the Trauma Crisis Centre when she qualifies.

Some would call the Trauma Crisis Centre at the time Chante arrived a *trauma-organized organization* – an organization that unconsciously arranged itself to defend itself against the enormous anxieties and challenges that trauma work brings with it. In the case of the Trauma Crisis Centre, the typical pattern was for staff to overwork and to become over involved with clients, and then to withdraw exhausted and hurt. This mirrors a common reaction people and communities may have to trauma – a lot of activity early on and then a sense of exhaustion, hurt, and withdrawal. In Chapter 7 we discuss more extensively some of the other ways that organizations can use to protect themselves against this kind of pain.

No magic cures

It is not always useful to reduce helping people to a series of steps or skills, specifically when helping others to deal with trauma. Though much training in working with trauma may be very helpful, there is also an enormous industry internationally in packaging trauma work as a set of skills and procedures which, if properly learned and religiously followed, will lead to recovery from trauma in clients. All over the world, there are courses in psychological *debriefing*, some of which are presented as a type of emotional first aid which must be administered if people are to survive trauma emotionally intact. There is in fact no strong scientific evidence that debriefing works – there seems to be about as much evidence for its working as there is for its not working, and even in some cases for its making things worse. This is not to say that debriefing cannot be helpful in some circumstances – there are many practices for which we have less evidence than we would like to have, and in all practices there is enormous variation, in client, caregiver, and context.

Given that the evidence for the success of debriefing is not impressive, why is there such a mystique around the area, and such emphasis on trauma debriefing as a very specialized set of skills and procedures? There are many possible reasons for this, not least of which may be economic – if debriefing is a specialized area, then those who have expertise in the area can make money by offering specialized interventions as well as by training others to do the work. In our experience though, most people who do debriefing and debriefing training are not cynical money-grabbers, and the profit motive cannot be anywhere a full explanation of their behaviour.

There is another interpretation for the popularity of debriefing and the mystique around it, which may be of more use for us in the context of this book. The idea of debriefing as a set of specialist skills that must be followed in all cases of trauma may in itself serve a defensive purpose. The idea of trauma, and the experience of it, may be so overwhelming that we wish there were some package we could use to prevent or cure the effects of trauma. We have seen how Chante seemed to wish Mrs Adams' and Donovan's problems to be small by referring to the murder as a 'slight upset'. Similarly, it would be wonderful if there were a magic set of trauma debriefing skills – the instant, magical cure is the bread and butter of many types of self-help programme and even of television chat shows. It is hard to accept the fact that trauma can have far-reaching effects (even across generations, as we have seen in both Chante's and Elana's case), and that we may be able to do far less than we would like in order to help. This thought, though, does not have to be entirely depressing. Recognizing our limits and the difficulty of the task – rather than falsely believing that we can do anything as long we have the magic technique – may be the most important basis we have for maintaining morale in the long run. This is a crucial issue as the burnout rates for people and organizations working with trauma are enormously high, and we must sustain ourselves and one another so we can continue to do the work.

In this chapter we have mentioned some aspects of trauma, which are unique to the field. Probably more important though, we believe, is recognizing that there is no clear boundary between trauma and other work helping people. Trauma work, first and foremost, is about listening deeply. It is also about recognizing the past in present reactions to trauma, about understanding relationships of all kinds, including those between caregiver and client. In short, trauma work is about all the principles we discuss throughout this book. It may also be the most important argument for a book of this kind – techniques, skills, and procedures may be helpful, but so is sustaining and caring for the people and organizations which look after people, often in very difficult circumstances.

Surviving our work with trauma

One of the biggest problems facing individuals and organizations dealing with trauma is burnout. We talk more about this in Chapter 7, but there are some issues specifically associated with trauma that are helpful to think about.

- Trauma *disorganizes* – it can muddle people up and interfere with their usual ways of coping.
- This disorganization can apply just as much to the traumatized person or community as to those who wish to help.
- Trauma *interferes with relationships and trust* – keep this in mind when working with traumatized people and do not automatically blame yourself if you find it hard to help.
- We all have traumas to varying degrees in our own past – if you can learn more about, and come to terms with, your own and your family's history, this can free you up to be more available to others.
- Allow yourself to feel exhausted and overwhelmed by trauma – when we accept that this is part of what trauma does to us, then we can take steps to look after ourselves and those with whom we work.
- Try not to take on too much – if you are completely overwhelmed and defeated by what you are dealing with, then you will not be able to do what is humanly possible to do.
- Look for signs that you or your organization are reacting badly to trauma and take steps to deal with this earlier rather than later.

CHAPTER 6

Culture and diversity

There are many ways of seeing and experiencing the world that depend on our up-bringing and beliefs. Having respect for another person's views without losing sight of our own core values can be challenging. We need to recognize both the differences and the similarities between groups of people.

Paul and Nosipho were colleagues working on a child mental health project in an informal settlement close to a large city. Paul was trained as a social worker at a nearby university; Nosipho was a mother recruited from the community to work directly with children and their families under Paul's supervision. Paul was raised in a working-class neighbourhood in the city. Although white, he regarded himself as closely aligned with the people in Nosipho's community, having shared a similar kind of poverty in his upbringing. At university, he learned Zulu in order to be able to converse with more of his fellow South Africans. Although Nosipho found it difficult in the beginning to accept that a man could have expertise about matters relating to children, she grew to respect Paul's energy, insight, and above all, his commitment to his work.

One day a mother who was very concerned about her four-year-old daughter approached Nosipho. The mother claimed that the little girl had been bewitched by her paternal grandmother. The grandmother had recently arrived in the city from a rural area and had, according to the mother, caused trouble in the parents' marriage and was bewitching the child. On hearing the story, Nosipho discussed what she should do with Paul. They both agreed that the first step should be for Nosipho to interview the little girl. Paul mentioned to Nosipho that in his understanding, witchcraft allegations are often used as a way of explaining interpersonal difficulties, and Nosipho agreed.

Nosipho saw the little girl alone. To her surprise, the child told her that she was kept with a large snake under her grandmother's bed, and that the snake regularly licked her whole body. At times, the grandmother would take her out from under the bed and they would fly around the township together. She said that she was not frightened of her grandmother or of the snake and that she was enjoying the attention.

On the basis of this discussion, Nosipho decided to interview the grandmother, although she felt quite frightened to do so. The grandmother was rather aggressive towards Nosipho, and said, "Don't forget, I am a witch. If you interfere with my family, you will regret it."

After this, Paul suggested to Nosipho that they present the case to a senior psychologist who visited the project monthly. When the psychologist arrived for his next visit, he had a visitor from Germany with him. The German visitor was to report back on the project to the German funders. When Nosipho told the story, the German visitor became very excited, saying that this was the first time on his trip that he was in touch with the real Africa, with the dark forces of witchcraft that dominate African people's lives. He claimed that there was only one way to help the little girl and her family and that was by getting in touch with authentic traditional African healers and asking them to perform an exorcism along traditional African lines. He said that he would like to witness this ritual, and to report back on it to the funders, who, he assured, would be very impressed that the project was being conducted in the real African way.

Paul became very angry at what the visitor was saying but did not want to say too much in case this would jeopardize the ongoing funding for the project. Paul thought privately that the visitor had a romantic, one-dimensional view of the community and of what it means to be an African. He pointed out that the project had not had good experiences with the indigenous healers in the area – they were expensive and had not done very good work. He was surprised and rather angry when Nosipho readily agreed to refer the matter to a traditional healer, agreeing that this would be the best thing. The supervising psychologist concurred that this was probably the best thing to do, but informed the German visitor that in African culture these rituals must be kept secret, so there would be no question of the ritual being observed by white outsiders.

After the meeting, Paul and Nosipho argued.

"How could you let that stupid German get away with all that racist rubbish?" Paul said. "He has all these silly beliefs about 'primitive Africans'."

"Paul, I feel frightened," Nosipho replied. "I suppose I'll do anything not to have to deal with this family."

"Frightened of what?" Paul asked.

"Of witches," Nosipho said.

"You can't be serious! You can't believe in that nonsense," Paul said incredulously.

"Don't tell me what to believe, and don't tell me about other people who are racist," Nosipho responded angrily. "You are worse than he is – not respecting my beliefs just because they are not the same as yours." Nosipho stormed out angrily, leaving Paul feeling confused and upset.

As we shall see later, the particular situation facing Nosipho and Paul was resolved in a helpful way, but it is useful to interrupt the story here to reflect on what their conflict tells us about our work.

Thinking about culture and difference

Increasingly, textbooks and training courses tell us that it is very important, when we work with people, to respect their cultural beliefs. People live their lives with different expectations, different ways of seeing the world, and different ways of making sense of both the good things and the bad things that happen to them. For a long time, people in the helping professions have been accused of not being culturally sensitive. At worst, different beliefs have been seen not for what they are – alternative ways of seeing and living in the world – but as a sign in themselves of problems. Consider the following example.

In many belief systems, in order to become a healer it is necessary to go through a period of emotional upheaval and upset first. In Zulu, this state is called *ukuthwasa*. The person who is going through a *thwasa* experience will often be very distressed and may behave very strangely indeed. To someone not familiar with this state of transition, the person may well look emotionally disturbed, and some writers in the past have, on the basis of this observation, claimed that African indigenous healers have emotional problems. What they have ignored, however, is that a *thwasa* experience, if properly handled, can be a successful part of a process of initiation into becoming a healer – and in fact, is a necessary part of becoming a healer. Throughout the world, shamans and healers are known to undergo similar experiences that in some cultures are seen as a period of being possessed by the spirits that are necessary for healing. Whatever one's own cultural beliefs, it is clearly a mistake to see this valued process of initiation into healing as something unwanted and undesirable.

Western authors at one time were very disparaging about beliefs held by other cultures. They regarded these beliefs as primitive and not as sophisticated as their own. In time, they argued, as people became more sophisticated and learned more about the world, they would abandon beliefs in spiritual forces, unseen things, and witchcraft. The Western world view was presented as scientific, and the highest point of understanding that there was. What was often ignored was that many very sophisticated Western people continue to hold spiritual beliefs – religious beliefs for example. Nowadays we tend to accept that almost everyone in the world holds some irrational or spiritual beliefs that are not based on scientific evidence. Even people who believe in science alone often do so on the basis of faith rather than logic – many of us, for example, travel on aeroplanes believing (we hope) that the aeroplanes will fly. We do this not on the basis of our understanding of aerodynamics, but on the basis of our trust, or faith, in the people who design and fly aeroplanes.

This all has very important implications for what happens to all people when bad things happen to them. When we fall ill, or we have problems in our relationships, or have trouble at work, or have any kind of difficulty that we would rather not have happen, we may look for a meaning for the difficulty beyond what we know about the scientific world. Many of us, if we fall ill at an inconvenient time, for example, may say things like this to ourselves, "It serves you right – you thought you could just carry on working and working, doing anything you like. This will cut you down to size." People often look for meaning in illness and misfortune in order to make some sense of what has happened and to take some comfort in this understanding. When a child dies, for example, a Christian person may say that the child was too good for this world, and that God needs the child to help with His greater plans.

It is important to recognize that these different views and beliefs exist to differing degrees in all people. It is not too difficult to accept this, as almost all of us can ourselves think about our own emotional reactions to upset and difficulty, and how we turn to such beliefs at such times. Accepting that there are many beliefs about the world and that no one has the single right answer to the world's problems – what is known as *cultural relativism* – is often quite easy in theory. In practice though, cultural relativism is hard to hold on to. There are also many reasons why people may wish to 'respect' other cultures – and these reasons may be complicated.

Culture, difference, and our feelings

Let's think now about some of Paul's reaction to the 'cultural' problem facing him, Nosipho, and their outside consultants. Paul has had a long commitment to respecting diversity but also to identifying closely with people who have been oppressed. He is worried about the ways in which outsiders will romanticize 'African culture' and make it into something fixed and mysterious. He believes that many non-Africans have used the notion of 'African culture' as an excuse to not get involved in working with African people. If 'African culture' is so different and impossible to understand, then non-African people are let off the hook – they do not have to get involved. In his particular project, he mistrusts the psychologist who visits monthly and then, as Paul sometimes comments cynically to his friends, travels all around the world telling everyone about the wonderful work he is doing in the African community. Paul has even less time for visitors like the German who, Paul thinks, represents a breed of people to whom the pain of the poor and oppressed in Africa is a form of travel show – a kind of entertainment. Who, after all, is this German visitor, newly arrived for a short visit to Africa, to say what the 'real' Africa is? What gives him the right to pronounce on what Paul and Nosipho do, and to turn it into a spectacle for his camera?

Nosipho, for her part, feels close to Paul and very loyal to him, but on certain matters – especially those of culture and language – she feels that Paul wants to gloss over the differences between them. She knows that it is important to Paul to identify with people in her community, but as much as she respects Paul, she can also see that he is not the same as her – even his involvement in this child project sets him apart (in a good way, she thinks) from many African men, who would feel humiliated by such work. Like Paul, she has little time for the psychologist who visits once a month and she is also tired of visitors who seem to treat her and her community like tourist attractions. But when the visitor speaks of African culture as mysterious and important, she agrees with him. There are things that outsiders cannot possibly understand, and she is glad that the visitor can see that. She also finds it very hard to explain to Paul that she is genuinely frightened by the grandmother-witch with whom she had to deal. Though she does not have very much faith in the indigenous healers in the area and feels that some of them are not genuine, she would be relieved to hand the case over to people more confident in dealing with issues of bewitchment than she is.

Nosipho and Paul both believe in respect for cultural diversity and they agree that imposing beliefs from the outside on a community is not a good idea. They agree further that all people turn to spiritual or non-rational beliefs when things are difficult for them. But Nosipho feels that Paul won't take her own cultural role seriously. As a younger African woman, she is already at a disadvantage when working with an older woman client, and she also feels intimidated by the powerful grandmother. She is unsure what to believe about witchcraft, furthermore, but she has seen some strange things in her time and does not want to take chances. She wishes that Paul showed as much cultural respect to her as he says he shows to members of her community.

Because Paul and Nosipho were good friends who also respected each other as colleagues, they were able to discuss the case and its implications in a more constructive way once they had calmed down. Paul was able to be persuaded that if the family believed strongly in witchcraft, then it would be an enormous advantage to them to have the help of a person who commanded respect among people with similar views. Nosipho agreed that if she worked alongside a respected indigenous healer with whom the project already had a good relationship, then it might be possible to offer the family the best help possible. The family were indeed helped – it emerged that there were conflicts in the family that could be worked with, and the indigenous healer dealt skilfully both with the mother's concerns about the child, and the grandmother's self-confessed status as a witch. Paul did not understand what had happened to help, but he could see that Nosipho and the family were satisfied with the outcome.

Nosipho and Paul were lucky that their good relationship carried them through the difficulties in which they were involved. Not long after this though, something happened to Paul that made him think again about the situation. Paul came from a committed Roman Catholic family. He had a long interest in liberation theology and was proud that his faith had led him to community service and to putting religious ideas into practice. He was not in favour of all the teachings of the church, and found the church's policy with respect to condoms and AIDS problematic, but on the whole, he believed that there was space for some diversity and dissent within the church.

Because of his concerns about the impact of AIDS on child mental heath in the community in which he worked, Paul contacted an HIV/AIDS prevention NGO to help him with AIDS education in the community. The workshops, aimed at people who care for children affected by HIV/AIDS, had in part, a preventative focus, providing education on safer sex practices. The facilitator from the AIDS prevention NGO was a young woman called Nomvula, and she worked in a dynamic and impressive way. At the end of the workshop, without having consulted with Paul, Nomvula distributed packets of brightly coloured condoms to all participants. Some of the people present, whom Paul knew well, looked shocked, especially the elderly women who formed the backbone of Paul's adopt-a-granny programme for abandoned and at-risk children. Some of these women had been recruited through the local parish of the Catholic Church. None of them complained, however, and they left quietly.

Once again, Paul found himself in an argument. He was angry both at not having been consulted about the condom distribution and at the action itself, which he felt was counterproductive in the context of what he had come to know as a concerned but conservative community. He feared that some of the older women with whom he worked would not wish to continue to participate in the programmes he had built up so carefully. He hardly knew Nomvula well but felt compelled to tackle the issue with her.

"Nomvula," he began, "I would have preferred it if you had consulted with me before giving out condoms at the workshop."

"I could see you were uncomfortable," Nomvula replied, "and I'm sorry about that but I don't ask people beforehand as the conservative ones say no and my business is to save lives."

"I don't think I'm conservative..." Paul countered.

"I can see you're a church type," Nomvula interrupted in a tone trying to make light of things, "probably one of those Catholic mission people."

"Yes, I am Catholic, but I am not conservative, and I know my community – these old ladies who help us out are all church women and they will react badly if you push condoms into their faces. Shouldn't we be trying to be sensitive to where they are?"

"Look, Paul, I deal every day with an epidemic that is killing my people. One in four women attending antenatal care is HIV positive. This epidemic knows no respect. I can't waste my time with 'respecting traditions' while my people die. And I can't believe that people like you still hold on to your religious mumbo-jumbo in the face of everything that is happening in communities like this. I'm sorry to be harsh, Paul, and I do respect your views, but if you want to help my people then you have to let go of these outdated beliefs of yours. African women are dying. This is the real world."

Paul was upset by this altercation but had to go to a meeting and so did not have time to discuss things further. He thanked Nomvula and stressed to her that he thought that the workshop was excellent in the main. They promised to have another talk, but were both secretly relieved that they had an excuse to part. Later in the day, Nomvula phoned to thank Paul for hosting the workshop, and apologized for becoming so angry. Paul appreciated this a great deal.

That night, Paul could not fall asleep. Was he just being conservative in the face of this epidemic he wondered? Were his own religious views simply holding him back? Without them though, he would not be doing the work in the first place. He knew the community he worked with – was he just protecting them unnecessarily? And what about this 'my people' business from Nomvula? It was clear that she had never been to this community, where he worked every day. Would he always be considered an outsider simply because of the colour of his skin? What gave her the right to talk on behalf of these people, whom he knew well? What gave her the right to trash Paul's own beliefs as mumbo-jumbo? What did she know about Paul's faith and his struggles with it?

Suddenly, Paul sat up in bed and, partly from exhaustion he thought, started to laugh. The last time there were any accusations about mumbo-jumbo and such things, he remembered, was when he became angry with Nosipho about the witchcraft incident. Now his own beliefs were being called witchcraft. "Serves me right," he chuckled, and went to sleep.

Insiders and outsiders

Paul's experience with Nomvula gives us another perspective on issues to do with culture and ways of seeing the world. From a perspective that is not his own, Paul's own religious beliefs can be seen as similar to witchcraft beliefs and can also not be understood from the inside. All people, no matter who they are, hold some views that will appear strange and even irrational or superstitious to others, and we need to take account of this when we provide services.

Layered on top of issues of cultural difference, though, are other issues which are sometimes more difficult to confront. In Paul's arguments with both Nosipho and Nomvula, there are questions about *insiders* and *outsiders*, and about who may speak on behalf of whom. Though Paul has always seen himself as part of the same political group as the community within which he works, he was shocked to find Nosipho talking to him as an outsider unable to understand the culture of the community. Nomvula, though she has not been to the community before, talks about 'my people', and Paul feels that she is implying that he is separate from these people. Past history and current racial politics play an important role in the way that people position themselves and others, in what comes to be seen as insider or outsider knowledge, and in how people should work. This particular incident was hurtful to Paul as he felt excluded unfairly, but there are at least two realities that he (and we all) must face. The first is that all sorts of people, and in different ways, will use ideas about difference to position themselves more powerfully than others. Men, for example, may say that women cannot understand their position, and deaf activists may argue that only deaf people can properly understand deaf language and culture. At different times, and for a range of reasons, differences will be emphasized and then de-emphasized. This can be quite bewildering to a person expecting consistency, but then again, none of us is completely consistent in our own identities – we change who we are and how we interact depending on circumstances. This is what makes us human.

If this first issue is about the ways in which difference is constructed and used, sometimes helpfully and sometimes not, there is also another level that may be even more difficult to think about. How possible is it fully to understand and identify with a person whose experiences are foreign to our own? In Paul's case, may there indeed be some limits to his capacity fully to 'get inside the skin' of a Zulu-speaking African woman living in a state of poverty? Painful though this may be, there must be some barriers, and it is probably much more helpful to recognize the possibility of these than to hope, through good intentions, political beliefs, or force of will, that these barriers will disappear simply by our wishing them away.

What, then, do we do in a situation not only when there are so many identities and ways of seeing the world, but also so many ways of making sense of all these identities, and of using ideas about difference in both helpful and unhelpful ways?

Accepting and processing difference

The first step is to recognize that differences do exist. These differences may change and shift, and, indeed they do, especially when people work closely and respectfully together. But if we simply assume that 'everyone is the same' we run the risk of ignoring what makes people people – their culture and individual identity. If we can accept that no matter where we work, and with whom, there will always be a time when we will be seen as an outsider, this makes it easier to realize that this process is not an individual one or our, or anyone else's, 'fault'. It is part of life and work as we must deal with it. It may be especially hard for people with strong beliefs about equality and democracy to agree that despite the fact that 'people are people' who share many things, there are also things that divide people. Those of us who come from countries with colonial or apartheid histories may feel especially uncomfortable with ideas of difference as it has been all too easy historically to use ideas about difference to oppress and subjugate people. But recognizing the possibility of difference is not the same as using difference as a weapon against people.

The second step along the way to working with difference is to try to recognize our own prejudices, beliefs, fears, and pride concerning issues of difference. Everyone is affected by issues of difference in their own way. One person, for example, may be very proud to be a Muslim, another may be ashamed to be a white man, a third anxious that people will reject her because she is a lesbian and so on. These investments in identity will affect us in how we interact with people. For example, it is very important to Paul to share a common identity with those in the community where he works – this may lead him to be especially sensitive when he is deemed an outsider.

If we are able to think about our own sensitivities about identity and difference, and about how these sensitivities may change or even appear and disappear depending on circumstances, then we can begin to look more clearly at what others are doing. Family therapists have a useful way of contrasting two ways in which culture can be used (DiNicola, 1986; Friedman, 1982):

> ***Cultural costume*** *is 'the particular set of recipes the individuals or families of a community have to give meaning and shape to their experiences and to communicate these experiences through shared ceremonies, rituals, and symbols ... When culture is invoked as a smokescreen to obscure individual states of mind or patterns of interaction in the family, the cultural costume becomes* ***cultural camouflage****.'*
>
> (DiNicola, 1986: 182–183)

What these authors are suggesting is that we need a more sophisticated way of thinking about culture than simply as something that people do or do not 'have'. We all have cultural beliefs, and respond to traditions and the ways in which we were brought up. But, consciously or unconsciously, we use these beliefs and traditions in different ways in different circumstances. Those of us who wish to help others need to be sensitive not only to the fact that differences exist, but also that differences may be used in a range of ways. In other words, we need to look both for the 'cultural costume' people may wear – the beliefs they hold and may have inherited about culture – and for the way in which these beliefs are used and not used for a variety of interactions. What the authors call 'cultural camouflage' can be said to be in operation when culture is used as a way of drawing attention away from, and even covering up, other difficulties.

An example of the shifting ways in which culture can be used both as costume and camouflage can be seen through the experiences of both client and counsellor in the following story.

A very religious Muslim woman, Bilqees, consulted Patience, a Christian trainee counsellor, because of concerns she was having about her child's unwillingness to go to school. It was obvious from the beginning that there were enormous differences between the two women. One of the first issues Patience had to deal with (and she discussed this at length with her supervisor) was her own reaction to the clothing worn by Bilqees, who was always completely covered from head to foot. With help from the supervisor, and from Bilqees herself, Patience was able to go beyond her feelings that this form of dress automatically created a psychological barrier between the two women. The relationship between them deepened, and though there were enormous differences between them in terms of how they saw the world, they were able to work together happily, not by denying their differences but by recognizing their commonalities. They were able to discuss very painful issues such as Bilqees's experience of abuse at the hands of her husband.

As the work progressed, however, Patience came to see that an important factor in maintaining and even encouraging Bilqees's child's refusal to go to school was that Bilqees herself felt lonely and frightened during the day at home, with all the family out about their business. Without being fully aware of it, Bilqees was giving subtle messages to her son that staying home to look after his mother was more important than school. She gave him special treats as soon as all the other children had gone off, and he had come to play a central role in her ability to cope with her day. This pattern of a parent subtly encouraging school refusal and, ultimately, making it hard for the child to return to school, has been shown to be a key feature of school refusal throughout the world.

Having recognized this common pattern, Patience tried as tactfully as possible to discuss it with Bilqees. At this point, and for the first time in the counselling relationship, Bilqees brought up religious difference as a factor hindering the work. "You've been very kind to me, Patience," said Bilqees, "but now I can see that you were right at the beginning. You will never understand Muslim ways and my religion, and especially what Islam says about the sacred relationship between a mother and her child. You have been very helpful, but I don't think we can go any further – I will be fine to carry on on my own now."

Patience was rather thrown by this, but had the presence of mind to ask Bilqees to come back for another session, if only to finish off things and end the counselling relationship. Bilqees agreed.

After Bilqees left, Patience felt quite unsettled by the session. Being rather inexperienced and being very concerned to respect cultural and religious differences, Patience went to her supervisor with the suggestion that she agree to end the counselling of Bilqees. As Patience and her supervisor thought about things together, though, it became clearer and clearer to both of them that, for whatever reason, Bilqees seemed to be using cultural difference selectively. Difference had not been a problem until now, but when the very painful issue of Bilqees's possible encouragement of her son's school refusal arose, suddenly, the cultural camouflage came up. Patience realized that if she did not point this out to Bilqees, she would be failing her client in that she would be colluding with this camouflage and participating in avoiding an important issue.

Patience felt anxious about the session to come. By way of preparation, she hit on the idea of contacting a well-known imam (spiritual leader) from Bilqees's community. Without giving away any details of the case (and hence not breaking confidentiality), Patience spoke on the telephone to the imam about her difficulty. The imam was very helpful, and agreed with Patience's supervisor that this was not the time to back off from offering to help the client, even though getting her to agree would be difficult. He offered to consult further with both Patience and the client, should this be helpful.

In the next session, feeling more sure of herself, Patience was able to point out to Bilqees gently how she had used religious differences selectively to keep the counselling away from the central, and most painful, topic.

Bilqees began to cry softly. "I can take anything about myself, you know, but what I can't bear is the idea that I am spoiling my child's life because of my own needs. This is every mother's nightmare, and look – I'm doing it."

"This admission takes great courage from you, Bilqees," said Patience. "I want you to know that I am here to help you with this and not to judge you. I have seen from how we have worked so far that we are able to find solutions together, and that is how we will work on this issue."

Hard though it was, the women were able to agree on a plan to change things for Bilqees and her child. As it happened, support from the community and from the imam in particular made Bilqees's task far easier. Her child went back to school and Patience supported her through the first stage of the loneliness, partly by continuing the counselling, and partly through helping Bilqees get over her shyness at

joining a Muslim women's religious and community work group. This group gave Bilqees an interest outside the home, gave her community support, and also gave her the chance to deepen her commitment to her beliefs. At the end of the counselling relationship, Bilqees joked with Patience that she had found to her surprise that she had needed a Christian person to show her how much more Muslim she could be!

The above story shows us how understanding the difference between cultural camouflage and cultural costume, and not being afraid to confront the issue, can help us help the many different types of people we work with. There are, unfortunately, also ways in which cultural camouflage has had serious effects on public health. When AIDS was first identified among gay men in the USA some of them argued that unprotected sex with many partners was part of gay culture and therefore could not and should not be challenged or changed (Shilts, 1987). Shilts argues that this factor, together with the refusal of the US government at the time (notably, President Ronald Reagan) to mention AIDS for fear of antagonizing right-wing religious groups, contributed to the spread of the disease. In both cases – those of the gay men and the Reagan administration – Shilts can be seen to be arguing that the idea of cultural difference or religious principle was used in a very harmful way. In sub-Saharan Africa, similar echoes are being heard. Some African men argue that it is part of their cultural identity as men to have unprotected sex with many women partners; others claim that this is an abuse of the idea of cultural identity, an abuse that is contributing to the worst epidemic in the world. On both sides of the debate, there are heated views – showing once again that culture is not a simple, static, or uncontested thing.

It is not always easy, therefore, to separate cultural costume out from cultural camouflage as they so often go together, but it is important to realize that just as we ourselves use ideas about culture, identity, and difference in complicated ways, so will the people with whom we work. We must recognize the complexity and not be silenced by it. Helman (2000: 82) raises the possibility that there may be cultural counter-transference – a complex of feelings about culture and difference we may feel towards people we work with; we can also think about cultural transference in the way people react to us. These concepts extend the ideas of transference and counter-transference we discussed in Chapter 4 as ways in which the past – our own, our clients' and our organizations' – lives in the work we do in the present.

We cannot get away from the differences among people, 'real' or 'imagined'. We also know that 'imagined' differences may be as powerful psychologically as 'real' differences. Part of our work is to take these issues into account and to allow them to help us make sense of the world. It is not necessarily a problem that there are differences – indeed, part of the process of containment (see Chapter 3) occurs when the person who acts as a container is able to keep a useful distance from others, and does not completely identify with them. Anthropologists have suggested that in order for work to happen, and happen well, we do not always need to understand perfectly what is happening across cultures. They speak of a '*working misunderstanding*'. This term is a witty change to the usual idea of a 'working understanding'. What the anthropologists are suggesting is that we should accept that it is not fully possible to understand another person's cultural beliefs. Indeed, every counsellor knows that it is not possible to understand every other person fully. If we accept this though, we can become more comfortable in realizing that whatever the differences may be, we may still be able to help up to a point. This is not perfect, but it is often very helpful. A 'working misunderstanding', properly understood, then, can be a basis for a helping relationship which both parties may recognize as imperfect and limited, but still one to be valued.

In this respect, the idea of a 'working misunderstanding' is similar to what the psychoanalyst D. W. Winnicott (1991) spoke of when referring to 'good enough mothering'. Winnicott, who worked extensively with parents and children, noted that though many parents strive to understand and handle their children perfectly, what is necessary is not perfection but being 'good enough'. Part of being 'good enough' involves being able to make mistakes and to recognize these and work them through in the parent-child relationship.

When confronted with the politicized and often painful world of culture and difference, we may often feel an internal pressure to understand things we do not fully understand. Many of us fear being called racist, sexist, ageist, homophobic, bigoted, xenophobic, or prejudiced in a range of other ways. In this context we may behave defensively by pretending to understand when we do not. It is all right not to know – any process of counselling is a process of discovery for both the client and the counsellor. It is surely far better to aim for a 'working misunderstanding' than for what can happen when difference is either not recognized at all, or is seen only as a problem. Where we as counsellors pretend to understand or cannot accept our limits when working with people we do not immediately understand, we can then have a 'non-working pretence at understanding'. This pretence, paradoxically, is far more prejudiced and problematic than any frank recognition of difficulties.

Thinking about culture and difference

Especially in countries where there has been a long history of institutionalized prejudice and racism, issues of culture and difference may be hard to think about. Here are some pointers that may help.

- Remember that it is equally true that people are alike all over the world and that people have different views of the world.
- Try to understand and be aware of your own cultural background – your upbringing, your beliefs, your values. Remember that even when we react against what we have learned and been taught we are influenced by these experiences.
- We all have prejudices. If you want to work around or against these prejudices, the first step is to understand them and accept that they are there.
- Allow for the possibility that others will see us and what we are trying to do from a different perspective. Even if others' perspectives seem wrong or misguided, they are a reality for those people.
- Don't be afraid to ask and find out about how others think, and to discuss differences – this is how we all learn and change.
- Accept that we will not all see the world in the same way – work together wherever it is possible but do not do things you do not believe in just because you think these may appear 'culturally acceptable' to others.

CHAPTER 7

Developing a 'thinking organization'

Human service organizations inevitably end up carrying the distress of their clients. It is important for organizations to think about how they are affected, and about how this can get in the way of their work.

Lindi worked full-time in an organization that offered counselling to rape survivors. She was an experienced counsellor and a pillar of strength in the organization as a whole. Lindi cared deeply about the women she counselled and was often very moved by their stories and their courage. When she wasn't counselling others, Lindi offered supervision and support to her colleagues and often provided a shoulder to cry on when they were feeling overwhelmed by some of the terrible stories they had to listen to. Not only did Lindi provide this formal support, but she was often also at the centre of a group of people in the tearoom who seemed drawn to her warmth and friendliness. As one of her colleagues explained to a new member of staff, "She's like the soul of this place. I don't know what we would do without her."

Lindi was very committed to her work and was often at the organization's offices long after her colleagues had gone home. "Someone needs to see to the emergency cases," she rationalized.

Everyone agreed, but privately several people expressed a worry that Lindi was working too hard and would not be able to keep it up. Over a period of several months, the organization found itself coming under pressure to provide a counselling service to a growing number of women who needed help. A clinic for adolescents that had operated in the area had recently closed due to a lack of funding, and this added to their burden. The rape counselling service staff found themselves taking on the difficult and distressing task of seeing more and more teenagers who had been raped and had nowhere else to go for help.

Lindi, being the kind of person she was, took on a considerable extra load. She sometimes counselled ten women a day and, as a result, found herself with much less time to talk to her colleagues. The other counsellors were also working hard and missed the support that Lindi used to provide. For a while, some of the younger counsellors still congregated in the tearoom, where they complained to each other that they felt tired and over-worked and that they no longer really enjoyed what they were doing. After some months of this pressure though, the tearoom was, more often than not, empty. People seemed to prefer to stay in their offices, finish their work as quickly as they could, and then go home. Staff members no longer met informally to chat at tea or any other time and a number of staff meetings were cancelled because the counsellors said that they were too busy to attend or were ill. The absentee rate was generally high among the full-time staff and a number of volunteer workers dropped out of their training programme in counselling. This of course put more pressure on those who remained to pick up the extra workload.

These issues came to a head for the organization when a staff meeting was finally scheduled and Lindi announced that she was thinking of leaving the organization. Her colleagues were shocked to hear her say that she was tired and didn't think that she could 'work like this' anymore. After a stunned silence, one or two other counsellors began to talk. One woman admitted that she also wasn't sure what the point was in carrying on. "It just seems like what we do is only a drop in the ocean. I don't see how counselling people who have been raped makes any difference if the laws don't change," she added.

Another woman agreed loudly, saying, "Yes, it's a waste of time if the police don't do their job and actually catch the rapists."

Soon everyone was talking in an angry way. After a while, one of the newer members of the organization spoke so softly that at first no one listened to her. When she finally managed to make herself heard, she said that although she hadn't been there very long, she could see that everyone was looking very tired from working so hard. "It's like we've been so busy looking after all these other people, we haven't been looking after ourselves," she added.

One of the other counsellors spoke up then, saying, "I suppose Lindi used to look after us and now, if she goes, we'll have no one."

The group was silent for a bit. Then Lindi spoke again, saying that she was sorry and that she hadn't meant to add to everyone's stress with her own problems. "In the end though," she pointed out, "we've all got the same problems with working too hard and feeling stressed. We need to find a way in which we can all support each other in the organization. Something's not right with the way we're working now and we've got to figure out what to do about it."

Those of us who are involved in helping others, often underestimate the extent to which this work takes its toll not only on us as individuals, but also on the organizations in which we work. In this example, it is possible to see how stress begins to affect not just Lindi, but the whole organization and everyone in it. In Chapter 5, we discussed the effects of trauma on organizations. In this chapter we will look at how stress affects the functioning of human service organizations more generally and suggest ways of trying to deal with this.

Now it often happens that organizations intuitively develop ways of managing stress. Many are lucky enough to have a person like Lindi, who plays a pivotal role in looking after people. In this case, Lindi not only takes on a considerable workload, but she also takes responsibility for supervising and supporting other staff. She does this partly because this is the kind of person she is and partly because the organization actually needs someone to do this job. There is no doubt that anyone doing a job as difficult as the one these people have to do, needs to have somewhere to offload their feelings. It is essential that new staff be supervised in their work and preferable that even more senior staff be given the opportunity to talk through difficult cases. It also seems right that staff should have a warm and friendly connection with one another and time to relax from the stress of counselling. People cannot be expected to manage difficult work like this if they do not have these sorts of outlets for their feelings. The problem in this organization is that a single person provides all of these vital supports. This makes for a very unbalanced kind of system, one that can easily collapse when there are additional pressures on either the person, or on the organization as a whole.

In this example, the organization is managing, but in a very insecure way that depends on Lindi alone to be there for the other counsellors. When the work pressure goes up, the staff become increasingly stressed and overloaded. Even more importantly, their main source of support, Lindi, no longer has the time to spend with them because she is already taking on much more than she can manage herself. Lindi is finding it hard enough to cope with her own workload, let alone be available to help the rest of the staff. In this very stressful time, staff are left without any back-up to help them carry on with their work. We can see how this begins to affect everyone in the organization. It begins quite slowly at first with counsellors moaning about their work and spending less time talking to one another. Then staff start to call in sick more frequently, volunteers drop out of the organization altogether, and formal meetings begin to be moved or cancelled. Finally, in the meeting, we see how despairing staff members have become and how they feel unable to believe that their work matters. They express anger towards the police and the legal system, but it is likely that they are also angry with Lindi for not supporting them, despite their awareness of her increased workload.

All of these things are common problems that take place in an organization when people are under stress. If this stress is not acknowledged and dealt with, it will begin to affect the work of the counsellors directly and inevitably, many staff members will start to think of leaving the organization.

Making a space to think in organizations

The signs of a stressed organization are, of course, much easier to see from the outside than they are when you are actually inside it. In the first place, things can often change quite slowly over a period of time so that you don't notice for quite a long while how bad things have become. More than this though, it is very difficult for people within an organization to see things objectively. When we visit another organization, however, many of us can quite easily spot potential problem areas. We may find ourselves wondering why they do this or that in one way when it would obviously be so much easier and better to do it in another. But when we become a part of an organization ourselves, our objectivity seems to disappear. We get used to things and everyone around us does too. Without even realizing it, we may find ourselves thinking along the following lines, "Oh well, this must be okay then. Things are just the way they've always been."

It is not surprising, therefore, that the people in our example take such a long time to realize just how difficult things have become for everyone in the organization. It is also not unexpected that the person who points out how tired and stressed everyone is, is someone who is relatively new to the organization. This is probably because she is just a bit more able than the others to see things from the outside. Because it is so hard to 'see' when our own organizations are struggling with their work, we have to try extra hard to think about what might be happening to us and our co-workers and to challenge our own beliefs that everything is the way it is supposed to be. It is useful for organizations to try and develop a collective habit of thinking carefully about how staff are managing and how this is affecting the work they are doing. It is equally useful to think of this job as belonging to everyone working there, who together can contribute to making a '***thinking organization***'.

Carrying the feelings of clients

There are very many things that can put stress and pressure on people and organizations and prevent them from doing their work properly. One of the most common sources of stress for human service organizations comes from the kind of work they have to do. There are few human service jobs that do not involve having to listen to and deal with people in distress. Whether you are a nurse in a hospital, a teacher in a school, or a psychologist working at a clinic, you are likely to be confronted with situations where people bring their worries and unhappiness to you in one way or another. In Chapter 5 we discussed how, when people are dealing with trauma, these feelings end up being transferred from the victim to the counsellor. This kind of transfer of feelings happens in all kinds of work situations, however, not just in 'trauma work'. The following example shows how care-workers can land up carrying all kinds of distressing feelings that they have taken in from their clients.

A children's home looked after the needs of the very young babies who lived there. A new childcare-worker who arrived at the home was put on the normal roster system where she was expected to look after four small babies who together occupied one of the rooms there. She had applied for the job because she loved babies and when the first baby began to cry, she picked him up and held him close to her chest, rocking him gently. Soon afterwards, hearing the cries of the first baby, a second baby began to cry. Still holding the first baby, she picked up the second with her free arm and began to quieten him. But of course, the third baby began to cry and then the fourth was wakened by the cries of the others. The childcare-worker tried to put down the first two babies in order to pick up the second pair, but this just renewed the crying of the two who had to be put down. Giving up on this method, the care-worker put all the crying babies into their cots and moved from one to another, patting them ineffectually and trying to quiet them with bottles. She became increasingly upset and panic-stricken herself and eventually simply sat down on a chair and waited for the babies to cry themselves into exhaustion, which they eventually did. Not surprisingly, the new childcare-worker was later found sobbing loudly in the toilet by one of the senior workers at the home. "They were crying and crying," she sobbed. "I felt so bad for them and there was nothing I could do."

What the childcare-worker felt in this instance is not so different to the normal communication that happens between a mother and a baby. A baby shows its distress by crying and the mother is meant to hear the cry and be mobilized by her own distressed reaction to go to the baby and soothe it. In the example, the care-worker responds appropriately to the children's distress with her own, but unfortunately finds that she is unable to comfort all the babies because there is only one of her and four of them. She is left feeling distressed and panic-stricken. In some ways, this is very similar to what many of us face in various kinds of care-work. We are given access to people's distress and we respond correctly with our own. Part of our job, though, is to be able to contain this distress in ourselves and so give the other person a chance to feel their feelings fully and to make sense of what they mean, as we discussed in Chapter 3. We should not, and often cannot, step in straight away to soothe people's hurt or take it away. The problem is that this often leaves us carrying some of their distressed feelings ourselves. This becomes particularly difficult when we have to cope with just too much of everything. Where we do not have the opportunity to let some of the feelings out, or to make sense of them ourselves, they can start to feel very overwhelming as they did for the childcare-worker in this story.

Given the kind of work that we do, it is natural that many of us will be carrying more than our fair share of our clients' distress. The counsellors who counsel rape survivors in the first story of this chapter, almost certainly leave their clients with fears about their own safety and perhaps are more cautious about locking their doors at night after hearing about a woman who was gang-raped in her own home. Nurses may find themselves carrying their patients' fears of illness or death and may dread their annual physical examination expecting to have their worst anxieties confirmed. Teachers may worry about their own children and how they are managing as they struggle to help a child who feels he simply cannot learn anything. Taking on these fears and anxieties is part of our job. As care-workers, we cannot really avoid these kinds of feelings altogether. When a whole organization is filled with people carrying very similar feelings of distress they will sometimes end up creating a work atmosphere that is dominated by these kinds of worries.

At a workshop for mentally handicapped adults, the staff had to watch the painful struggles of a group trying to manage and complete the work contracts that helped the organization to survive financially. The handicapped adults were involved in doing quite simple tasks like wrapping various goods or cutting sheets of paper for which they and the workshop were paid. But often even these basic tasks were beyond their capabilities. The staff felt terrible watching as the handicapped men and women grew increasingly distressed as the deadline for the completion of a job approached and they became more and more clumsy in their attempts to finish on time. The staff, however, seldom talked about this particular aspect of their jobs, feeling that it was so much a part of things that it couldn't be changed. Instead, over the time that the contracts were being completed, staff began to accuse each other of incompetence and an inability to do their jobs properly. The atmosphere in meetings was intensely critical as each in turn made the others feel stupid, useless, and ashamed of themselves. This behaviour only stopped when an outsider pointed out to them that their actions seemed designed to make each other feel just as bad as their handicapped clients.

In this example, the feelings of the clients are not only carried over into an individual staff member, but also begin to be a part of the way in which people relate to each other. In the same vein, organizations that deal with teenagers may find themselves acting in very childish ways. Those that deal with victims of abuse may find that people are unusually suspicious of one another and alert to the possibility of being taken advantage of. The important thing to bear in mind is that people working in any organization should try to keep thinking about the feelings they have to face on a daily basis and how these might get inside them and indeed inside the whole organization. Sometimes organizations find that the feelings their clients bring them are too difficult to manage at all, and devise ways of trying to avoid them. Although initially helpful, these avoidance tactics sometimes end up getting in the way of either people doing their jobs properly or getting satisfaction from their work.

Going back to the example of the children's home, the new childcare-worker soon discovered that the other staff members there had found a unique way to protect themselves from the kind of distress she had felt when she listened to the babies cry. What she learned was that the staff had made a decision that no one should be allowed to pick up the babies unless it was to feed them. There was no really rational reason for this rule and it seemed to have been developed simply to protect the staff from feeling upset when they couldn't pick up a crying baby who needed to be comforted. "Well, it's not allowed, is it?" they could simply say to themselves, and after a while this would help to block out their distress about the crying. The problem with this though is that it started to get in the way of people actually enjoying their work. Most of the staff, like the new childcare-worker, had gone into this work because they cared about babies. Now they were trapped by a rule that stopped them from getting close to their charges. Deprived of the emotional warmth of cuddling a small baby and stuck only with bathing, changing, and feeding, a number of the care-workers became increasingly disillusioned with their work. Blocking off their distress in this way was understandable, but it also robbed them of a chance to look carefully at the system of care they had set up and to maybe find a more realistic way of organizing the work roster. Ideally, this should have allowed two child minders to be on duty together which would mean that the babies could indeed be picked up and comforted as they cried.

When the stress an organization faces is too great for it to manage, people unconsciously begin to look for ways of blocking out the painful feelings. This can be helpful, for example, in the case of an emergency worker who needs to shut out his distress so that he can attend calmly to the job of freeing someone from a car wreck. However, when protective measures are used thoughtlessly or in inappropriate circumstances, they can become a greater source of difficulty than the original problem they were intended to address.

To avoid this unconscious cycle of distress and protection, it is important to be able to recognize and identify the particular ways in which your job might be stressful. This allows the problems to be recognized, named, and if possible, addressed. The difficulties for some organizations might be that they have to listen to the distressing stories people tell them, while for others it might be that they have to be involved in distasteful tasks such as bathing and cleaning sick people. In other cases it might be difficult because there is nowhere to get away from the continuous demands of clients, or perhaps that the organization itself is located within a violent area of the city and there are concerns for the safety of staff. Some people think that talking about these things would encourage a kind of unhelpful 'moaning' attitude among staff but in fact, the opposite is almost always true. When people are able to voice these concerns and talk through them they often feel better able to manage them. Also, while it is not always possible to prevent the experiences that give rise to these difficult feelings, there are sometimes small adjustments that can be made to the work environment or routine that can ease some of the difficulties.

Extra stresses for human service organizations

In addition to the work itself, there are also other things that cause stress for those who work in human service organizations. There are few countries in the world where the human services available seem adequate to meet the needs of the people. Most of us work in situations where there are more clients than we can cope with, where the demands on our time are more than we can manage, or where it feels as though there is always something else to be done. Inevitably, this leaves most organizations with the experience that they are not doing enough. Some organizations try to manage this feeling by taking on more and more, as in the next case.

A local mental health organization working in a gangland area, found, not surprisingly, that one of the biggest problems for its clients was the high level of violence in the neighbourhood. The organization was doing good work in the community, offering an on-going counselling service as well as all kinds of other opportunities for social and recreational activity. In the face of continued gang violence though, the organization felt that it was making no inroads into the 'real problem'. In response to this, it decided to shift its attention away from mental health issues in order to start a nation-wide peace project. Staff put a lot of energy into this work, but eventually it became clear that the project was too big for a small, locally based organization to address effectively, and that in fact, staff did not really have the skills to put many of their ideas into effect. During this period, the organization had allowed the counselling and other aspects of its original work to collapse and when staff realized their mistake, they struggled to get these going again.

This sort of response to what seem to be overwhelming needs is very common among organizations. As a result, organizations often end up taking on more than they can manage. A small health organization may set the unrealistic goal for itself of turning around the AIDS epidemic. An educational project may want to provide remedial help to every school in its area, despite the fact that it employs only two remedial teachers. While of course it is important for organizations to think creatively and positively about what they can offer, when they feel they have to give more than they realistically can, staff members are often left feeling disempowered and useless. It is more helpful for organizations to recognize the limits of what they can do, and to try and do whatever they can within these limits as well as they can. Setting realistic goals helps staff to feel motivated and to keep going even when things are difficult.

One of the biggest sources of pressure for many organizations working in the human services is financial survival. All around the world governments are cutting back on the amounts of money they give to education, health, and social services. Various organizations are being expected to survive on much less than previously, or to try and raise additional funds for themselves. Just as it does in a family, continuous worries about money can often make other problems and conflicts feel much bigger than they are. It can also feel particularly difficult to experience the lack of these basic kinds of resources when you feel you already have to give so much of yourself to your job.

There is no way of getting away from these kinds of stresses, but like all problems, they tend to feel more manageable when they can be spoken about and acknowledged. Many organizations are developing innovative ways of raising extra funds, but most people involved in human service organizations have not had training in financial management. It is helpful for organizations to acknowledge that they may be working under difficult conditions and to allow themselves the time to develop the necessary skills they need to survive.

The organization in trouble

There are a number of warning signs that indicate that an organization is under stress. Some of these were described in the first example in this chapter of an organization offering counselling to rape victims:

- Staff members often lose the enthusiasm they once had for their work.
- They seem to lack the energy to take on new activities and many start to miss work, either through genuine illness or a reluctance to be there.
- Sometimes an individual staff member who started off his or her career with high hopes for themselves, takes on too much and eventually begins to suffer from what is called *burnout*.

When an organization is under considerable pressure for long periods of time, many individuals begin to feel stressed. As an air of dissatisfaction spreads through the organization, it becomes contagious and even new members are quickly 'infected' with feelings of hopelessness. Inevitably, the work of the whole organization begins to suffer. The feelings of hopelessness start to seep into people's attitudes with their clients, who become pulled into a kind of shared pessimism. In this atmosphere of gloom, people find it very hard to remain motivated and they often lose touch with their own abilities to change things. It is not unusual to find staff of an organization in this kind of state waiting around hoping for someone or something to rescue them, without recognizing that they have the power to correct things themselves.

It also often happens that organizations under a great deal of stress may find themselves dealing with a lot of angry feelings. As people see their organization seeming to lose direction, and as their jobs no longer give them satisfaction, they may find themselves feeling angrier and angrier. It is natural for people in this state to look around for someone to blame. Often it is the leader of the organization who is seen to be responsible for the organization's difficulties, but sometimes conflicts erupt between groups in a random way. In both cases, the morale of the organization may be further damaged. Sometimes people find someone or something to blame outside of the organization. This is perhaps what happened when some of the counsellors started talking about the police and the legal system in the first example in this chapter. This can work for a short while to distract the organization from its own troubles and briefly make people unite together against an outside 'enemy'. However, this kind of response does not, in the end, help people to recognize their real difficulties or to take responsibility for changing circumstances for the better.

What is burnout?

Burnout is a recognized syndrome affecting people in the helping professions. It is the term used to describe the effect that prolonged over-work has on people. People who are vulnerable to burnout are those who give too much of themselves to their work and who do not know how to take care of their own needs. If they do this for too long a time, they start to experience a whole set of problems including:

- exhaustion;
- lack of motivation;
- loss of job satisfaction;
- resentment of the tasks and people associated with work;
- isolation from colleagues; and
- illness.

Developing coping organizations

We have sketched a very bleak picture of how organizations respond to stress. Many, of course, do not find themselves in such terrible circumstances. Most, hopefully, recognize potential difficulties and begin to deal with them before they start to seriously affect the organization's functioning. Just like people, organizations have the potential to be stressed, but also the capacity to be resilient and to cope with the difficulties they have to face.

One of the most important factors that improves an organization's ability to cope with stress is the amount of support it can offer to its members. As we saw in the first example of this chapter, it is not helpful to only rely on an informal system of support that can fall apart if one person is not available. Ideally, support should be built into the structures of the organization itself, and the task spread across a number of people. There should be some kind of supervision available to junior or new staff members from members who are more senior. More senior people should also have the option to talk with their colleagues on a regular basis. As we have shown in this chapter and others, this kind of talking is not a luxury in human service organizations; rather it is essential if the organization is to manage its work effectively. It is also useful to have some kind of 'open door' policy that allows people to chat to a senior member of staff outside of their allocated supervision time. When working with the needs of distressed clients, it is often most useful to be given the chance to let out difficult feelings as soon after a session or encounter as possible. We know from trauma work that the time factor is important and having immediate access to a sympathetic listener can prevent the need for much lengthier help at a later stage.

Informal support is also very important in an organization. We all work better when we like our colleagues and have a sense that we form part of a supportive team. It is not as difficult to improve the quality of relationships in the work place as one might think. Often, simply arranging a regular teatime during which other activities cannot be scheduled makes a big difference to the ways in which people get along with one another. Bringing cakes on the Friday after a particularly gruelling week can also do more for staff morale than many complicated organizational development exercises.

Of course, it is also important to make a space for all members of the organization to meet together to discuss their work more formally. In terms of developing a 'thinking organization', this is vital. It provides the opportunity to review the way that the work is going, to look at difficulties people are experiencing, or to readjust the aims of the organization if needs be. It is important nonetheless, that the formal talking space is still space for real talking. It so often happens that staff meetings get bogged down in bureaucracy or are dominated by a single person or group. In these cases, the real talking may be done outside the meetings in the passages and behind people's closed office doors. This creates the possibility of unhelpful divisions and conflicts in the organization.

When open discussion doesn't seem to be able to happen within normal meetings, it may be useful to schedule a special ongoing get-together set aside only to talk about how people are feeling. Sometimes this is called a 'staff support' group. A number of mental health organizations offer a staff support group to their members that is facilitated by a skilled person from outside the organization. Although this might seem like a luxury to people who are used to working under a lot of pressure in various community settings, it can prevent stresses from becoming overwhelming and actually save time and money for the organization in the long run.

A second very important must for a coping organization is a good system of authority. Many human service organizations seem a bit uncomfortable with the idea of authority. Perhaps this is because those who work in these organizations are so tuned in to listening and following their clients that they struggle to see themselves in more active roles. Often authority is also associated in people's minds with negative ideas about the abuse of power. But a strong, solid, and reliable system of authority operating within an organization can often provide the 'holding' that people need in order to manage the anxiety that is generated by their work. This does not have to be in the form of a rigid or controlling leader who makes no space for people to explore their own ideas or ways of doing things but rather has more in common with the idea of containment that we introduced in Chapter 3. Organizations work best when there is a sense that someone or some group is capable of holding things together in a flexible way. This is especially important when things are difficult. Much like a young child who needs a routine and a sense that an adult is watching over him or her, an organization needs structures, routines, and people who can take charge of aspects of its functioning as the need arises.

Most importantly, a coping organization is one that can think its way through its problems. We hope, of course, that our clients will be better able to manage their lives by acknowledging the reality of their situations, however painful, by having an opportunity to reflect on their experiences, and by seeing how things need to be changed. Similarly, an organization needs to allow itself the same opportunities to name and understand its difficulties and to explore what these mean for people. This increases the organization's capacity to withstand stress and, where possible, to make changes to its functioning that allow it to take better care of its members.

Being part of a thinking organization

- Take some time to think about yourself and your own needs – not just those of your clients.
- Recognize the stressful nature of your work.
- Learn about how your organization works and what particular kinds of stress you and your colleagues have to deal with.
- Help both yourself and the organization to set realistic goals – be careful not to take on too much.
- Try to identify the strategies your organization uses to protect itself from emotional pain and explore whether or not these get in the way of the work.
- Help develop good systems of formal and informal support for yourself and your colleagues.
- Develop strong leadership within the organization so that they can protect and support all staff.
- Help yourself and others to keep challenging and re-thinking the accepted ways of working within the organization.

CHAPTER 8

Dealing with change

Coping with change and transition is a major challenge people face today. The kinds of changes we have to deal with are many and complex. This chapter looks at the ways in which people respond to change. It offers some advice on how you can cope with change and help others do the same.

Andile comes to the city

Andile, a twelve-year-old boy, recently arrived in Durban from his home in Melani, a rural village, to stay with his mother. Andile was born in the city, but was sent to Melani when he was four. Andile was brought up by his grandmother, but was sent back to the city when she became ill. Andile's grandmother was strict and very protective. Her discipline was harsh and she believed that children should simply listen and do what they are told. Despite her strictness, she was kind. Andile had had fairly infrequent contact with his mother, as she would travel to Melani each December. Three others lived with Andile in the Durban house – his mother, his sixteen-year-old sister, and his aunt. Every now and then his mother's boyfriend would sleep over. His elder sister and his mother argued often; about the music she listened to, about how late she stayed out at parties, and about whether or not she studied hard enough.

Andile had been excited about coming to the city. He looked forward to spending time with his mother. She'd always brought him presents in December and he'd thought that there was lots of money in the city. He knew that his grandmother didn't have enough money and this worried him. Nonetheless, Andile secretly hoped that there would be more than enough money in Durban and that he wouldn't have to worry about this any more.

The city turned out to be a very different place to the village where Andile had been living. "Life is so different," he thought often to himself. Everything seemed so much faster, bigger, and busier to him. Although he entered the same grade at school, the work was different and he started to feel that he didn't understand anything. He began to think that maybe he was just stupid.

Andile tried to make new friends, but he found the boys in the city to be very tough. Even the ones his age seemed older than him. Several boys in his class smoked marijuana and talked a lot about sex. He wasn't used to this. They used slang words that he'd never heard before and he felt ashamed that he didn't know what they meant. He saw some boys bullying other boys and girls and he started to feel scared that they would bully him too. Andile began to hate the mornings. He felt anxious and nauseous. Andile heard about other children skipping school and thought that maybe he should too; he was scared of getting into trouble because he wasn't doing his work. Andile thought a lot about his grandmother and his home in Melani. He wished he could be there with her again.

Andile's mother was stressed. She needed to get up very early to catch two taxis to the city centre, where she worked as a cleaner. She worked a full day and after changing taxis got home after six at night. She worried constantly about money. She'd been sending money to her mother, but now that her mother had fallen ill, she was even more worried about her. She had noticed that Andile was

becoming withdrawn, but she told herself that because he was a child he would adapt. She felt that she had too much to juggle; her daughter fought with her all the time, she was always worried about money, she had to look after Andile, and now her mom was ill. She felt it was all too much. She sometimes woke early in the morning crying.

Andile is facing many losses, changes, and challenges. He has lost the support of his grandmother. He has lost his friends. He has to make new friends while trying to adapt to a new school and a different way of teaching. He needs to adapt to a new subculture. He needs to adapt to a new kind of relationship with his mother. The adjustment that Andile is facing is enormous. How can we begin to understand the different ways in which Andile is trying to cope? Examining the concept of stress is a useful way of thinking about how people cope with change. That Andile is under stress seems obvious. Let us examine how the concept of stress relates to Andile.

Change and stress

The concept of stress is useful in helping us understand the ways in which people respond to changes and transitions. Stress is a person's response to a stressor, an event that provokes some sort of reaction. Stress takes two basic forms – eustess (positive stress) and distress (negative stress). Stress is sometimes an important and necessary component in helping us deal with challenges. It can provide us with the motivation or the energy we need to tackle an obstacle and in this sense, it is positive. Sometimes, though, stress can be harmful, especially if it makes us feel overwhelmed or if it continues for too long.

We all have a certain capacity to deal with change. Should an event occur which is outside of our capacity to cope, then we become stressed. Changes are often stressful because they stretch our ability to cope. In fact, changes almost inevitably make people feel stressed. Andile is struggling because the things that he has to deal with are beyond his ability to cope.

The fight or flight response

Dealing with change is stressful. When we are stressed, our bodies react in a very particular way called the fight or flight response. We literally get ready to fight or to run away. This response by the body involves a general increase in heart rate, blood pressure, and respiration. Stress hormones and adrenalin are released in the body and our blood sugar levels increase. Our muscle functions heighten, our senses become keener, and our digestion is suppressed. Our bodies become primed to respond to a challenge. This response is adaptive, because it gets us ready to take some sort of action. Andile's nervous feelings and nausea in the mornings could be part of this sort of stress response.

Acute and chronic stress

The fight or flight response may occur in response to a single event such as an argument or nearly being involved in an accident in the traffic. This is termed acute stress. It gets us ready to act, to respond. We are able to take evasive action, to get out of a situation, or to fight and stand up for ourselves. Acute stress is short lived and our bodies usually return to a normal state fairly quickly. This happens all the time and is in fact an adaptive and motivating state. However, should this state endure and become chronic stress then it may be problematic. Chronic stress is stress that just doesn't stop. Andile's mother is under chronic stress – the things she worries about just don't seem to get better. Chronic stress depletes the resources of the body. Acute stress can turn into chronic stress if the stressed person is unable to deal with the stress or if the stressful event persists. Sometimes the meaning of a stressful event is such that the person can't come to terms with it, as in the case of a severe trauma, for example. Signs of chronic stress include tension headaches, prolonged fatigue, sleeplessness, irritability, depression, feeling overwhelmed, and a decrease in concentration.

It is important to look at the stress response in detail. If we are familiar with the signs of stress, in ourselves or in those with whom we work, this can provide us with a useful warning sign. It is useful to sometimes reflect on whether we are experiencing any of these signs ourselves. Should one be experiencing the fight or flight response in an ongoing way, or the signs of chronic stress, then it is important to do something to try to deal with the situation.

The personal meaning of stress

An important part of why changes are stressful concerns the meaning we attach to them. Some things that might stress one person, might not stress another. The reason for the difference lies partly in the meaning that a stressor has for different people. The way in which we make sense of things that happen is crucial in affecting whether we are stressed or not. Clearly, there are some events that are stressful for all people, such as major disasters. However, even in these situations, the ways in which we cope with the stress (in other words, whether we survive it or not) depend on the meanings these events have for us. In other words, our memories, beliefs, and attitudes affect the meaning of an event and hence our ability to cope with it. If we think we have lost control, we are more likely to experience increased distress. Particular events are likely to evoke memories of prior similar events. If we experience a disappointment with a loved one, it may feel very similar to a disappointment we felt with an important person in our past (for a full discussion of this process, see Chapter 4 on transference).

What makes a difference to how we cope with change?

Many things make a difference to the ways in which people cope. It is useful to think of them in three categories:
- factors to do with the person;
- the availability of social support;
- the nature of the change.

The way in which these three factors work together is the key thing in influencing how we cope with change.

Factors to do with the person

Feeling in control

One of the most important factors influencing how we cope with change or stress is the degree of control we feel we have over the things that happen in our lives. If we feel that we are able to influence events, we will feel that the things that happen are under our control and we will not feel helplessness. Having a sense of control lessens the feeling of threat. In order to retain the feeling that we are in charge of the things that happen to us, we might utilize coping strategies that reinforce this feeling. We might, for example, reinterpret events, telling ourselves as we do so that an event does not mean anything. We might rationalize that we chose the event and so can cope with its attendant stresses. Having things organized and structured is often important for people to feel in control. If people know how their day or week works and what they can expect, it can make them feel in control. This is why planning a week and knowing in advance what we want to do can help us feel more in control. If routines change it can be unsettling.

Our inner resources

Inner resources are those aspects of ourselves that we bring to a situation. One of the things that we can bring to a situation that will help us cope with change is our health. If we are fit we have a greater capacity to deal with stress. Exercise also uses up the adrenalin and stress hormones in our body, helping us to return to a normal state more quickly. This is why exercise is so often recommended as a way of dealing with stress.

Another aspect of our inner resources concerns our ability to manage, understand, and think about our feelings, or our *internalized container* (see Chapter 3). If we have survived experiences of frustration in our past, and have been helped to understand our feelings in a way that makes us feel in control, then we are more likely to cope and to feel we can have control in the present. In other words, if we have a strong sense of self-esteem and confidence we are more likely to be able to cope with stress. Our internal resources also include the skills and adaptive strategies we have learned. If we have dealt with change before, we will have a sense of how we respond to it, and what dealing with change takes.

In our example, Andile is trying his best to cope. However, it would be hard for any child to cope on his or her own with the kinds of changes Andile is facing. Another way of saying this is that while Andile is trying his best, his inner resources are not sufficient for him to cope on his own. Often people think that children are adaptable. While this is true, children also need help in order to adapt. Little children especially find it hard to adapt to change, particularly if their principal caregivers, those to whom they are most closely attached, are absent.

The availability of social support

Andile clearly needed some support in adapting to these major changes. A major influence on whether or not we are able to cope is whether or not we have support from others. A large-scale research project in England showed that not having social support played a major role in whether people became depressed or not (Brown and Harris, 1978). The kinds of support that people need include:

- tangible and practical support (someone to help share the load);
- informational support (someone to provide us with information about

what our options are) or network or community support (where we are part of a community which pulls together to provide us with help);
- emotional support (people who help us deal with and think through our feelings and who make us feel valued, who boost our esteem, and who make us feel secure).

One of the most powerful sources of support comes from a close relationship with those to whom we are attached.

Attachment and its importance in sustaining esteem

If we have a close and supportive relationship with significant others, we are able to feel more secure and in control during times of stress. While it is particularly true for children that having a close attachment figure helps them to deal with change, it is the same for adults. Brown and Harris's (1978) study also showed that people can be protected from depression by having a supportive relationship. Brown and Harris called a close supportive relationship a *protective factor.* During times of change a person to whom we are attached can provide us with a sense of safety, security, and belonging. When we form an attachment to someone, it provides us with a feeling of security and safety. This is partly why counselling feels supportive – apart from the problem solving or working through that might occur, the person forms an attachment that allows a feeling of security. The attachment can form the basis of an alliance, or a working partnership. We feel that together we can deal with something.

Of course, where previous attachments or relationships have involved problems, there may be fears that the same problems will occur again (in other words a transference may occur – see Chapter 4). The feeling of attachment allows us to be able to work through fears and worries about the relationship. We may develop a fantasy of how someone will help us and this will keep us together. The thought of how things will be on returning home may be enough to sustain the motivation of someone far from home.

Part of what is hard for Andile is that he has lost a major attachment figure – his grandmother. His mother is trying to cope with her own problems and seems to find it hard to think about what Andile is facing. She expresses a hope that he will adapt, but is struggling to be a support for him. Andile finds himself thinking a lot about his home in Melani, wishing he could be there with his grandmother. When he thinks of his grandmother he is thinking of a time when he felt safer. Thinking about her helps him to feel a bit better, but also makes him sad. He does not have anyone to help him think about and manage his new experiences. He is missing a container.

The containing function of support
When confronting a new situation that involves having to learn and adapt to new and unfamiliar demands, we may need the help of someone who can help us think through what we are facing – we may require a container. Having a container allows us space to think. If we can put our worries into the jug that the other provides, we are able to think more clearly and feel more secure. Knowing that help is available can be enough to help a person find the strength to deal with tough challenges. This is what Andile needs.

The nature of the change

The last factor which influences how a person will respond to change is the nature of the change. Nicholson (1990) has described several dimensions of change that are important to consider. These include:

- the speed at which the change occurs (in other words, does it happen quickly, leaving us little time to prepare?);
- the size and complexity of the change (does it demand a lot because it involves so much?);
- the importance of the change (will it affect our lives greatly?);
- whether the new state has any meaningful connection with the previous state (can we make sense of the new demands by relying on our experience, or are they totally new, thus leaving us completely inexperienced?).

If we are confronted with something we did not expect, something very complex and serious that we have never had to deal with before, then the demands placed on us will be much greater.

How these three factors work together

The way these factors work together is what is important in shaping whether or not someone copes. This is what is hard for Andile. He has lost a major attachment figure, a major source of support – his grandmother (and so is dealing with issues of loss), he has come to a new and strange environment (there is a lot for him to adapt to), and his mom is overburdened (there is little support for him). This is a massive amount of change for anyone to cope with. It is no wonder that Andile is feeling helpless, scared, and homesick.

Adjusting to change

The cycle of adjustment

Nicholson (1990) has suggested a model for understanding the processes and phases that people go through in adjusting to a change. This model is useful in giving us clues to the different needs that people may have when confronting changes and stressful events.

Stage 1: preparation

The first stage in the cycle is that of *preparation*. This is the stage when people make themselves ready for a change. Adequate preparation is crucial if someone is to deal with change. People who know that something is going to occur may have many hopes, wishes, and expectations. There may also be many fears about the coming change or event. Anticipating a change often leads to a great deal of anxiety. The person may be reluctant to undergo the change, particularly if the change is not desired or if the person does not feel they understand the change, or if they have not had a role to play in deciding how the change will happen. In fact, even when changes are desired, people may still feel reluctant to change.

Andile had a lot of hopes about what coming to the city would be like. Part of what is so hard for him is that the city is so different from what he expected. He desperately needs someone to help him adjust, someone to help him think through all the things he is facing.

Sometimes it is hard to prepare for a change. It seems that what we feel about the change is wrong somehow. An example of this is the difficulties people have in talking about becoming parents. People often have many fears, resentments, or doubts regarding the birth of a child. They find it hard to discuss these feelings with others because pregnancy is so highly valued in society. It is hard to acknowledge that something that we and others feel should be a positive experience, is in fact difficult for us. We may feel that others will judge us and so we feel ashamed to seek support. Our difficulty in discussing these feelings may also involve our own guilt and our own worry that we are somehow abnormal to be having them. (In fact, these sorts of feelings about childbirth are very common.) If one is working as a counsellor, it is important to validate people's feelings as a first step to helping them work through them. It is better to acknowledge the feelings than to pretend that they do not exist. Denying what we feel creates its own tension.

Stage 2: encounter

The second phase is that of *encounter*, when we actually begin to face the change or event. It is during this phase that our expectations are confronted, and we come to see if what we expected really occurs. During this phase our emotions are likely to be heightened and we may enter the fight or flight response. Our perceptions will be sharp. Feelings associated with this stage may be excitement and joy if we have looked forward to the change. It is often the case that things do not go the way we planned. Should things be different from what we expected, we may also feel shock, regret, or fear. At this point we may be thrown back into anxiety and a feeling of helplessness. This is what was happening to Andile. The city was just not what he had hoped for. He started to feel that he didn't know what to do.

It is important to remember that for many people part of coming to deal with a task includes feeling helpless or anxious. While they are working out what to do they may feel disorganized or out of control. If we have adequate support and a sense of our ability to survive, we may be able to move beyond this feeling (which is about us trying to come to terms with the experience). Also, people may come to recognize that this is how they always feel when dealing with change, and can then tell themselves that they know it will get better. If we lack support, however, the feeling of being unable to cope may overwhelm us and we may start feeling that we cannot get on top of the situation.

One of the most important things that support provides us with is the knowledge and belief that we can get through stressful situations. If we feel like we have failed, it is often very important to try again. If we cope with something by avoiding it, then often the next time we encounter a challenge we will avoid it again. We then build up a fear of the thing we have to do. It is therefore sometimes important to go back and try again. As the proverb says, 'if you fall off a horse, get right back on'.

Stage 3: adjustment

The third phase is that of *adjustment*. In this phase the person's task is to adapt to the new environment and learn the new social rules of the situation (in other words, to come to know what is expected of them). If things go wrong, the person may feel like a misfit and may start to feel bad about themselves. At this point the person may be confronted with a great sense of loss, as they grieve the things that they miss.

Stage 4: stabilization

The fourth phase is that of *stabilization*. In this phase, if things have gone well, the person will know what is expected of them and will come to perform adequately. Things will settle for them. There should be a return to a previous functioning to some degree. If things do not go well, the person may feel a sense of failure and helplessness. The person may start believing that they are not capable. Andile is in danger of reaching this stage, should no one help him to adjust.

The ways in which people confront the different tasks at each stage of the cycle depend on their internal resources, their feeling of control, the availability of support, and of course, the nature of the change or event that they must face.

Coping with ongoing change

Change happens all the time and so we are all likely to be in many cycles of adjustment at any one time. Change also often happens quickly and we may have to encounter a change and perform at the same time. Or we may feel we are in the encounter or adjustment phase all the time, without time to prepare or to stabilize. In situations of ongoing change we may feel that just as we think we have reached a point where we know where things are going, things change again. We may feel like we never reach a point where we know what to do.

Nicholson (1990) provides a set of useful questions that we can ask ourselves or others when dealing with changes:

1. Where am I now on the transition cycle?
2. How did I get here?
3. Has there been a pattern to my experience of previous change cycles? Do I respond to change in a similar way?
4. Are there warnings in these patterns for how things will go now?
5. Can I foresee where the cycle is going next?
6. Is there something I can do to determine what happens next? Can I control it?
7. Who can help me in this and other phases?

Asking these sorts of questions helps us make sense of where we are and gives us a greater sense of control. It also helps us to think about whether or not we need to ask others for help. Remember, having support is one of the biggest ways of protecting ourselves from the stress of change. Sometimes we may need to take a risk to ask for support.

Endings

Let us now turn to look at one particular kind of change, that of loss and grief. Losses of all kinds – bereavement, separation from a loved one, divorce – produce a wide range of feelings in people. When they are responding to loss, people will in many ways go through the cycle of adjustment we have just described.

Working with people who have lost others can be difficult for counsellors. Seeing people in this sort of pain is especially hard. It makes us think about our own losses and we may feel helpless as a result. In addition, working with loss may stir up our own fears about death. If as counsellors we are still battling with our own losses, working with others who are mourning can be very painful. We may find ourselves remembering loved ones we have lost. The principles that we have explored in this book about listening empathically, seeking to understand our own feelings and thereby coming to understand and contain the feelings of others, and about seeking out the help of others to manage our feelings, will stand us in good stead in helping us to come to terms with working with those who are grieving.

Mourning and grief

People's reactions to loss are very varied. The kinds of responses that people go through when they lose someone have been described often, but it is useful to describe them again. We must remember that not all people go through these stages and many people will have feelings and thoughts from several stages at one time. If we can understand the kind of response to the loss a person is showing, this will help us decide how best to help them.

The phases of grief can be understood as part of a person's struggle to come to terms with a loss, to make some sort of meaning out of it. If the person can develop a satisfactory account of the cause or meaning of the event, then they may be better able to cope with it. For example, someone may tell himself or herself that it is okay that a loved one has died because their time had come. What is important about the way a person makes sense or meaning is not whether this is objectively true, but rather if it makes sense for the individual.

The stages or kinds of feelings that people go through when facing grief are as follows:

- *Denial and isolation*. In this part of the reaction the person finds it very hard to accept the loss. They may act as if nothing has happened, or tell you that they don't believe that the loss has occurred.

- *Anger.* In another stage, the person will express anger about the loss. They may feel angry with themselves, the dead person, or with others.
- *Bargaining.* In this stage the person tries hard to soften the blow by fantasizing that things could maybe be different, if they did something. For example, people may find themselves praying, trying to strike a bargain with God to bring someone back.
- *Depression.* In this part of the reaction, the person realizes that the person is gone and becomes very sad, sometimes withdrawing from others.
- *Acceptance.* In a final stage, the person has come to terms with the loss and life returns to normal to some degree. Sometimes this can take many years. Often the pain of loss never really goes away, but people get better used to dealing with it.

Complicated grief

Sometimes it is hard to grieve. We may find it hard to let someone go, or the grief may be too painful for us. When this happens to someone, we say that their grief is complicated. Communities with HIV/AIDS, for example, face repeated losses. People often have to mourn entire families. People's sexual and intimate relationships, through which they have experienced closeness and security, are disrupted, and they are forced to find new ways of being intimate. Since each person has to face a disruption of bonds of attachment, and also has to consider his or her own mortality, it may be very difficult to go through mourning. Individuals with HIV or AIDS may feel isolated and have difficulty re-engaging with their relationships, families, or communities. They may remain angry, embittered, and withdrawn. We need to understand that mourning is hard for them. Letting themselves mourn may force them to confront their own death. It is very important at these times that care-workers understand the individual's fears and why it is hard to mourn.

Ending a working relationship

Ending a working relationship, such as that between a teacher and student, or counsellor and client, can be painful. In these sorts of relationships bonds can often become strong, and the ends of these relationships often remind people of other losses they have felt before. Ending work relationships can thus evoke transference reactions (see Chapter 4). Whenever a helping relationship you are involved in comes to an end, make sure to think about what the end of the relationship means for the person you have been helping. People may become angry, sad, or may want to find a way to thank you. It's important to help people through such an ending. Endings are often an opportunity to help a person come to terms with other losses that they have experienced. Helping people deal with endings can be difficult because the feelings that we need to manage in ourselves are often powerful. Let us look at an example of where an ending, in this case not a final one, brought up feelings about prior losses for a child.

Alex is fourteen years old. He was raised by his aunt because his teenage mother could not look after him. Alex found it hard to get on with others in his aunt's home, where he was the youngest of six children. His aunt had little time for Alex, whom she resented having to look after. When Alex was nine he was caught stealing. Around this time he began to be disruptive in class and his teachers found him increasingly hard to handle. He always seemed to be looking for attention. When he was eleven, Alex was caught vandalizing a toilet in a mall during a school outing. His teachers were very angry with him and his aunt decided to send him to a boarding school. At the boarding school he was initially very quiet, but he soon began to be disruptive in class again.

Around this time Noteko joined the school as a care-worker. Her task was to look after the pupils in the afternoons. Noteko had been raised by her grandmother and so she felt that she understood what it was like for the children at the boarding school to miss home. The students at the boarding house liked Noteko. She was firm with them, her rules were usually clear, and she still took the time to understand them.

Noteko immediately noticed Alex. It was hard not to, as he always seemed to be in trouble. Noteko and Alex began to talk every now and then and eventually he seemed to form quite an attachment to her. Alex would come to her office after school and the two would chat about his day. He always seemed very eager to tell her about what he had done and Noteko felt that he always tried to impress her.

Some weeks after Noteko joined the school the holidays came around. Alex's aunt informed the school that she was not able to take Alex for the holiday. As the end of the term drew closer, the children in Alex's dormitory made plans to go home. The head of the boarding house told Alex that he would not be leaving. When Alex spoke to Noteko about the holiday, however, he told her how much he was looking forward to going home. Noteko became worried. Alex did not seem to have accepted the fact that he wasn't going home.

A few days before the end of term, Noteko and Alex were talking. Noteko told him again that he would not be going home, but that the school was trying to find another home for him to visit in the holidays. Alex looked up at Noteko and asked, "Could I come and stay with you?"

Noteko felt very sad for Alex. She knew it was the school's policy that children could not go home with staff, but she felt that if she told Alex this he would be very disappointed. At the same time, she felt very protective of him and wished she could take him home. "We'll see," she replied.

Alex looked happy and went off to his room. Noteko was worried and checked to confirm plans that Alex could go home with another boy. When this was certain, she decided to tell Alex the news. She told herself that he would be relieved. This is how she broke the news:

"Hi Alex," she said, "I want to talk to you about where you are going to go for the holidays."

Alex looked very excited. "I can't wait to go!"

Noteko felt anxious, but plucked up the courage to tell Alex the truth. "Alex, actually, I'm sorry, you can't come with me, but..."

Before she had a chance to finish, Alex started shouting. "You don't care," he said, "you're just a loser like everyone else!" Alex stormed out of the room.

Noteko got up and followed him as he ran out onto the playground. As Alex ran he began to cry.

"I'm just going to run away. I'll look after myself," he said to himself.

Noteko finally caught up to him. "Alex, wait, what's wrong? I've got good news, you're going with Mario".

"Mario is an idiot. And so are you," snapped Alex.

Seeing how angry Alex was, Noteko realized that she had been wrong in not being honest with him from the start. "You really wanted to come and stay with me," Noteko offered quietly.

"Yes! Why can't I? You are just the same as everyone else. You don't care!" Alex was now sobbing. Noteko sat next to him. She knew how painful it was for him.

"I know it's disappointing, but that's the rule Alex. Pupils can't go home with staff".

"That's not fair!" he wailed miserably.

Endings are hard for Alex

Alex became very angry with Noteko when he found out that he could not go home with her for the holidays. He had formed a close attachment to her and had developed a fantasy that he would go with her for the holidays. He wished that Noteko could look after him. When Noteko told him he wasn't going home with her, this fantasy was shattered. The disappointment Alex felt with Noteko clearly parallels his disappointment in his mother and aunt. Alex feels that no one cares for him, that he is always being let down, and that his only option is to look after himself. In Alex's eyes, no one is to be trusted.

There was thus a transference of these feelings to Noteko. Noteko initially kept striving to make things better for him, but that was impossible. Alex had already been hurt. Later Noteko came to realize how painful things were for him and she made a comment to him that reflected this understanding.

Sometimes it is hard to help prepare people for endings because the endings are so painful. If we feel guilty in some way, or if the loss evokes our own memories of losses, we may find it hard to bear the feelings the other person has. We may also try to take the feelings away, to make it better for them. In reality, we often cannot make it better. One cannot take away the pain of those who have lost people. Making false reassurances to people that their pain will go away is also not helpful.

Dealing with endings

The first half of this chapter offered some advice on helping people prepare for changes. The points discussed are also very useful in helping people deal with endings. As in all work with others, if we can come to understand our own responses to others, our counter-transference, we will find it easier to know what to do with others.

There are no perfect endings

There is often no perfect way to prepare a person for an ending. When things end, people seldom feel that everything is finished. As a counsellor who is saying goodbye to a client, we may wish that the person's issues were resolved, but this is not likely. However, we may have started someone on a new road that will take them to a better destination than the one they were headed for before they came to us. But we often cannot say what that destination will be.

Sometimes it is hard when an ending is abrupt and we feel unsure about whether or not we have helped someone. Sometimes we may have a strong need to help (which may be part of why we do this work in the first place). This sort of need affects how we see endings. We may find it hard to let clients go. Noteko felt something similar to this when she tried to make things better for Alex by at first not telling him he could not come home with her. Alex had already been hurt and no matter what Noteko did, the end of term was bound to be painful for him. Noteko realized that Alex needed to be prepared for the end of term, but found it hard to help him do this because she sensed just how difficult it was going to be for him.

Alex finds it hard to deal with endings. They make him feel upset and out of control. He tries to make himself feel in control by telling himself that he will look after himself. However, he really doesn't feel like he can. If Alex has an opportunity to work through his disappointment and if others do not repeat his trauma, things may in time become different for him. He may come to learn that people can be trustworthy.

What do endings mean?

Help the person explore what the ending means for them. Let the person talk about what the ending means. If it is an ending of a counselling relationship, it is likely to evoke strong feelings. People may feel grateful, sad, or angry. As we have said, an ending is likely to remind people of other endings in their lives, so sometimes we will have to manage the transference (see Chapter 4). In other words, we will have to act in a way that is best for the person, based on our understanding of what their past has led them to need. For this reason, it is very important for Noteko and the school to be consistent.

Bear with the ending

Sometimes all that we can do is be there for the person to talk to. Sometimes what someone needs is to know that there is someone there. We may be able to do little more. At this point we will have to contain the powerful feelings that this will leave us with in order to be able to bear just sitting with someone.

Support and supervision: helping you cope with endings

Working with endings can be very painful. Because of the amount of pain we may have to bear on another's behalf, we will need our own source of support. This will involve getting supervision in our work to help us understand our counter-transference, as well as getting our own emotional support. As we have seen, having support is one of the most important things that helps people cope. As someone who's role it is to help and support others, you too deserve a pillar of your own.

Helping people prepare and cope with changes

Helping people think through and talk about the things they are about to face can help them feel more prepared, whether the changes are adjustments, losses, or endings. Having a space to talk out their feelings about a change can help give people a feeling of control. This may be the first time that they have put their fears and hopes into words and it is likely that this will help them gain some perspective. It will also help them feel supported.

Preparation will not necessarily take away feelings of anxiety, but may help the person have a greater sense of control. Also, there will always be things that the person cannot have anticipated. Let them know that feeling anxious is normal.

While preparation beforehand is important, as the person encounters the new situation they may need ongoing support. Where appropriate, set up follow-up meetings. One discussion may be enough, but more may be needed. If the person knows that they have a space where they can return to talk, it will help them feel contained. If the person is at a later stage of the adjustment cycle (encounter, adjustment, or stabilization) they may also need to explore questions similar to those presented below.

Questions to ask a person preparing to cope with change

The following points should be woven into the discussion with the person. If one lets the person talk about the things they are facing, it is likely that they will cover many of these points, but you may need to address some of the following issues to help some people talk:

- Ask a general question like, "How do you feel about this change/event?" Let the person talk in his or her own words about the change.
- Think about the degree to which the person has control over the change. Is there anything the person can do to be more in control? Are there practical steps the person can put in place to help them prepare? Are there things they must do? Can the person think about these?
- When discussing with people how to cope with adjustments it is very useful to consider helping them think about the kinds of support they need and how they can go about getting that support. Who can they tell about their problem? Who should they tell? Are there reasons why they are scared to tell others? What plans can they make to get help from others? Who can they ask for specific help?
- Think about the nature of the change that the person is facing.
- What do they know about the change or event?
- What are their hopes? You might ask something like, "What is the thing you most hope for?"
- What are their fears? You might ask, "What is the thing you fear the most?"

- Ask about what they know about the nature of the change. When will it happen? How will it happen? What does it involve? Have they had any experience with something similar? What new things will they have to deal with?
- Can the person tell you about what they feel are the next steps? This lets them rehearse the change as much as possible beforehand.

CHAPTER 9

The world of our work

There are many challenges facing the people of the world today. These include illness such as HIV/AIDS, widespread poverty and inequality, voluntary and involuntary migration, and soaring rates of violence and injury. In order to make a difference in this rapidly changing environment we need to understand and respond to the human dimension of global problems.

Readers who have got this far with this book will probably be people who have an interest in, and a commitment to, human service work. This work is often not recognized (it is often described as invisible), is seen as 'soft' or 'easy', and is poorly paid, if it is paid at all. Most of the work of supporting others, furthermore, is not done by people who are in jobs that are there in order to provide this support in the first instance. Much of the burden of caring for illness, disability, and the effects of violence is borne within families and communities. Traditionally, though this is by no means always the case, women have picked up a large part of the load of caring, in addition to all their other responsibilities. Teachers, police officers, health workers, even hairdressers and bartenders, cannot avoid being confronted with human pain and suffering. In this book we have tried to make the implications of this explicit, but the issues go far further than self-help in helping others emotionally. A broader social change is needed which recognizes the work and the context that creates it. We need to rethink the limited definitions we have for who provides psychological support work and what this work is.

There are many stereotypes about doing work that supports people psychologically, and most of these are not very helpful. These stereotypes include:

1. Only people with serious psychological problems need emotional support.
2. Psychological difficulties are a luxury that only some people can afford – only the rich get depressed.
3. Only professional counsellors and psychotherapists can offer psychological support.
4. Managers and co-workers are wasting valuable work time if they offer support to colleagues.
5. Psychological well-being is not relevant to health, education, economic activity, and physical development.
6. Psychological support and well-being are relevant only in western countries – they have no meaning in Africa, Asia, and the rest of the world.

As we have already seen through the stories in this book, these statements, and others like them, are not true, even though they may be quite commonly expressed. There is increasing recognition, however, that psychological factors are absolutely central to all people's well-being and development.
One way in which researchers have tried to measure the human cost of disease and injury the world over has been through The Global Burden of Disease and Injury Series, a very large project run jointly by the Harvard School of Public Health and the World Health Organization. According to the Executive Summary of this large study:

> *The next two decades will see dramatic changes in the health needs of the world's populations. In the developing regions where four-fifths of the planet's people live, noncommunicable diseases such as depression and heart disease are fast replacing the traditional enemies, such as infectious diseases and malnutrition, as the leading causes of disability and premature death. By the year 2020, noncommunicable diseases are expected to account for seven out of every ten deaths in the developing regions, compared with less than half today. Injuries, both unintentional and intentional, are also growing in importance, and by 2020 could rival infectious diseases worldwide as a source of ill health.*
>
> (Burden of Disease Unit, Harvard School of Public Health, 2000: 1)

The authors of this report have developed a way to measure disease burden that they term *Disability Adjusted Life Years* (DALYs). According to this measure, major depression (known as unipolar major depression) ranked fourth in the world in 1990 as a cause of disease burden, after respiratory infections, diarrhoeal diseases, and conditions arising during the period shortly after birth. Using known scientific data and methods, they have also developed a projected ranking of what may be the leading causes of disease burden worldwide in 2020. The top fifteen diseases or injuries, in rank order of contribution to burden, are shown in the box below.

Rank order of disease burden projected for the year 2020, measured in Disability Adjusted Life Years (DALYs)

1 Ischaemic heart disease
2 Unipolar major depression
3 Road traffic accidents
4 Cerebrovascular disease
5 Chronic obstructive pulmonary disease
6 Lower respiratory infections
7 Tuberculosis
8 War
9 Diarrhoeal diseases
10 HIV
11 Conditions arising during the perinatal period
12 Violence
13 Congenital abnormalities

14 Self-inflicted injuries
15 Trachea, bronchus, and lung cancers.

Source: Baseline Scenario Figures from *The Executive Summary of The Global Burden of Disease and Injury Series* (Burden of Disease Unit, Harvard School of Public Health, 2000: 4).

If we look at the list of projected causes of disease burden in the box above, we can see that not only are there conditions that are commonly accepted as psychological problems or their consequences (for example, depression and self-inflicted injuries), but also that behavioural factors are influential in all conditions. For example, war, violence, and road traffic accidents are all affected by human behaviour and aggression in particular; the spread of HIV and tuberculosis depend on social relationships and the way these are negotiated; smoking and alcohol consumption are major risk factors for many of the conditions listed and so on. Behavioural and lifestyle-related issues are not luxuries that only the rich can afford. On the contrary, they affect our societies and the future of our planet in serious ways.

What does this mean for those of us who choose to work with people? This book is evidence of a beginning of social change in the way key policy-makers view the importance of mental health. In 1995, for example, Desjarlais and his colleagues published the *World Mental Health Report*, which demonstrated the importance of mental health issues for low-income countries across the globe. They were able to show how closely mental health issues relate to other social issues – such as, for example, gender equality and massive migration – and how mental health problems are both a consequence of and contributing factor to poverty and underdevelopment.

Perhaps even more significant than the *World Mental Health Report* is that the World Health Organization dedicated the year 2001 to a mental health focus. Mental health formed the basis for discussion at the ministerial round tables at the World Health Assembly held in Geneva in May 2001, and the annual *World Health Report* for 2001 focuses on mental health issues. It is also relevant for this book that the *World Health Report* for 2000 focused on health systems research, and recognized that an important factor in the improvement and maintenance of health systems is how these systems will succeed or fail in addressing the needs of health service providers.

In the rest of this chapter we will consider some of the social challenges facing the world, and the developing world in particular, and the implications these have for psychological support work. We have chosen to focus on the four areas of HIV/AIDS, poverty, violence and injury, and migration not because they are the only important areas facing the developing world, but because together they give a broad sense of some common issues.

HIV/AIDS

According to the Joint United Nations Programme on HIV/AIDS (UNAIDS), at the end of 1999 there were 34.3 million people living with HIV/AIDS worldwide, with 24.5 million of these in sub-Saharan Africa. Of the 1.3 million children under the age of fifteen living with HIV/AIDS throughout the world, 1 million were in sub-Saharan Africa. In 1999 alone, 2.2 million people died of AIDS in sub-Saharan Africa. There were approximately 15 000 people newly affected with HIV every day in 1999, and 95% of these new infections were in developing countries. The biggest age category at risk is the most sexually active population (fifteen to twenty-four years), and by the end of 1999, there were a total of 13.2 million children orphaned by AIDS worldwide – 12.1 million in sub-Saharan Africa. The Burden of Disease Unit of the South African Medical Research Council (Dorrington *et al.*, 2001) estimates that in South Africa in the year 2000, approximately 40% of adult deaths (people aged between fifteen and forty-nine) were due to HIV/AIDS, and that AIDS is now the single biggest cause of death in South Africa. The authors project further that without treatment to prevent AIDS, by the year 2010, between 5 and 7 million South Africans will have died of AIDS (Dorrington *et al.*, 2001: 6).

The implications of this for those concerned with human welfare are enormous. Let us list just some of the ways HIV/AIDS has an impact on our work, and some of the challenges posed to us. The list is by no means comprehensive, and it also covers some areas that do not obviously have anything to do with the epidemic, but are affected profoundly by it.

Issue	Challenges
AIDS prevention work	No proven means of AIDS prevention known; human behaviour change difficult; time gap between infection and becoming ill large, so health education and promotion difficult.
Community-based AIDS activism	Stigma in discussing sexual matters; community denial, threats of violence; other priorities in communities.
Support for HIV-infected people and people living with AIDS	Stigma and rejection from communities; working with loss.

Working with AIDS orphans	Lack of resources for placement; dealing with loss and grief.
Health care for people not infected with HIV	Health system in difficulties over increased load of HIV/AIDS patients.
Staff development work in large organizations	Staff illness and death owing to HIV/AIDS; loss of skills in workforce; impact on workforce dynamics.
Community policing	Safety and security affected by AIDS-related illness and death in the community.
Poverty relief work and job creation	Increased patterns of illness and death have economic and human consequences.

In all these areas of work, there are profound emotional challenges both for the public at large and for the service provider. If we are to avoid burnout and uncaring attitudes towards the community, the issues that we have discussed in this book must be taken into account in work affected by HIV/AIDS.

The burden of poverty

There are 6 billion people in the world. Almost half of these (2.8 billion) live on less than US$2 per day, and a fifth (1.2 billion) live on less than US$1 per day. Of the world's very poor, 44% live in South Asia, and 24% live in sub-Saharan Africa. The absolute number of poor people is growing fastest in sub-Saharan Africa. The infant mortality rate in this region is fifteen times that of high-income countries. The average income in the world's richest twenty countries is thirty-seven times the average income in the world's poorest twenty countries, and this gap between rich and poor countries has doubled over the past forty years (World Bank, 2001: 3–4). Even within countries, there are enormous gaps between rich and poor. In 1991, for example, white South Africans enjoyed a standard of living comparable to those living in what are termed High Human Development countries, whereas black African South Africans were at the low end of the Medium Human Development scale. The Western Cape Province of South Africa, similarly, fell into the High Human Development category, whereas the Northern Province of that same country fell into the Low Human Development range (May, Woolard and Klasen, 2000: 24). The World Bank has developed an index known as the

Gini index – a measure of the degree of income inequality within a country. For a long time, South Africa was recorded as having the world's highest Gini coefficient (May *et al.*, 2000); according to the latest World Bank figures[1], the highest recorded Gini indices are for Sierra Leone (62.9), Central African Republic (61.3), Brazil (60.0), Guatemala (59.6), and South Africa (59.3), where the richest 10% of households have a 46% share of all income and consumption in the country, and the poorest 40% of households have among them only an 8.4% share (World Bank, 2001: 282–283). An important feature of all these countries, not surprisingly, is a high rate of social instability through war, criminal violence, and similar phenomena.

Given the fact that poverty is so widespread and the gaps between rich and poor both within and between countries so extreme, many would argue that all efforts should focus on eliminating poverty. In this view, psychological and social support issues become luxuries that do not deserve attention. There is an increasing recognition, though, that if the consequences and eradication of poverty are to be adequately addressed, we cannot ignore the human consequences of, and contributors to, ongoing poverty. Introducing the *World Development Report* of 2001, the World Bank notes:

> *Poor people live without fundamental freedoms of action and choice that the better off take for granted. They often lack adequate food and shelter, education and health, deprivations that keep them from leading the kind of life that everyone values. They also face extreme vulnerability to ill health, economic dislocation, and natural disasters. And they are often exposed to ill treatment by institutions of the state and are powerless to influence key decisions affecting their lives. These are all dimensions of poverty.*
>
> (World Bank, 2001: 1)

Poverty and inequality are so entrenched that the important long-term agenda of eradicating poverty must be accompanied by work that looks at what poverty is and does to people, and how this feeds again into a cycle of poverty. As the above quotation shows, poverty brings with it a series of social consequences, including personal powerlessness and humiliation, and no scheme that ignores these dimensions will assist people to break out of the trap of poverty. We are reminded of an organization that provided business skills

[1] The figures for different countries have been collected in different years and using slightly different methods, so they are not directly comparable. For our purposes though it is sufficient to note that there are countries with enormous discrepancies between rich and poor.

training in a very poor community. The training seemed to go well, but a year later not one of the people who had received the training had made any attempt to start a business. Part of the difficulty was that the recipients of the training were so demoralized and lacking in confidence that they could not, without ongoing emotional support, take the risk of developing new business ventures and, indeed, new identities for themselves.

It is by now well established that there is a close relationship between poverty and psychological difficulties. Poverty may have an impact on mental health, and mental health problems may in turn lead to problems with earning money. Patel, Araya, Lewis, and Swartz (2001) have illustrated the vicious cycle of poverty and mental health problems using the diagram shown in Figure 1.

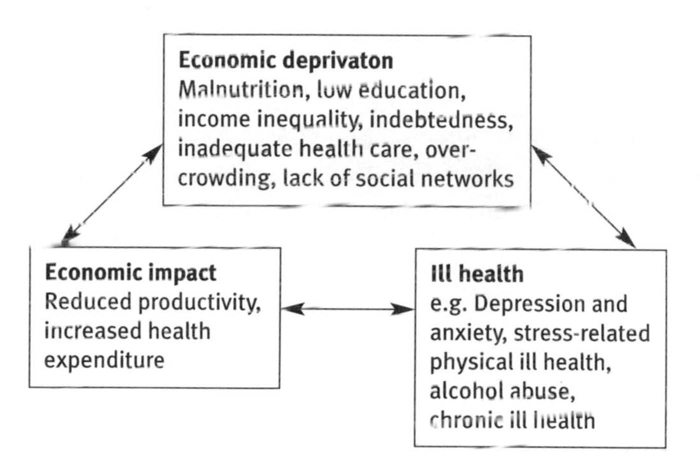

Figure 1 *The vicious cycle of impoverishment and mental disorder*
(adapted from Patel, Araya, Lewis & Swartz, 2001).

Dealing with poverty, and attempting to prevent it, then, is a very complex task with many components. People who provide human service support to very poor people often carry an extra burden in their work, and this is the burden of living every day with the economic gap between the provider of support and the poor community being served. Very often in our own experience and in supervising others we have been faced with the same dilemma: does what we do, as social service workers, mean anything at all to impoverished people? Would it not be better simply to give money to poor people who need it? Would it not be better if instead of accepting our salaries we gave the money over to poor communities, and found some other way to sustain ourselves? What can emotional support mean when people are struggling to survive? These are all legitimate questions that demand careful thought, and cannot easily be swept aside. In fact, in our ongoing work with poor people these questions never go away – they return and have to be thought about again and again in different contexts.

It is also true though that the dimensions of poverty are so large and complex that reducing poverty is never just a matter of money. As Budlender (2000) notes in her discussion of malnutrition, the problem is not simply medical but also social, political, and economic. Social and political development and change depend not only on money but also on human skills in accessing resources and organizing communities, and it is in this area that we can make a difference. Even helping impoverished parents with childcare and supporting them to provide the best they can for their children in terms of emotional support for learning can have significant economic benefits for families and communities in the longer term.

There is, in summary, a great deal that we can and should be doing to intervene in the vicious cycle of poverty, demoralization, and psychological difficulties. In order to sustain ourselves though we need to have support – support that recognizes both the value of the work, and the fact that the work is demanding and endlessly challenging both ethically and emotionally.

Violence and injury

Violence and injuries constitute a major and increasing public health problem worldwide. In industrialized countries, violence and unintentional injuries (accidents) are the main cause of death in the one- to forty-year-old age group (World Health Organization, 2001: 1). In most countries, accidents are among the leading causes of death. Injury and violence are among the leading causes of disease burden internationally, and this pattern will grow (see the information box on page 124) to the extent that it has been estimated that by 2020 intentional and unintentional injuries could rival infectious diseases as a source of ill health (Burden of Disease Unit, Harvard School of Public Health, 2000: 1). The terrorist attacks in New York on 11 September 2001 highlight bewildering changes in patterns of violence and injury. When, during peacetime, thousands of people can be killed through terrorism in a single day, and in the conflict that ensues, this profoundly affects how we all see and experience the world.

Each day, almost 16 000 people across the world die from injuries; many more are injured and some are permanently disabled. Patterns of injury vary markedly according to socio-economic status and from country to country. People in Africa, for example, have war, interpersonal violence, and road traffic injuries among leading causes of death, whereas in the Western Pacific road traffic injuries, drowning, and suicide are prominent. In wealthy countries in the Americas, the leading injury-related cause of death among fifteen to forty-four year olds is traffic injuries; in the poorer countries in that region, the leading cause is interpersonal violence (World Health Organization 2001: 3). More than 2 million people die each year as a result of violent attacks, and many more are disabled. Socio-economic status, gender, and age are among the factors that led to different vulnerabilities to violence. Women, for example, are more likely than men to be sexually assaulted; men are more likely to be both perpetrators and victims of firearm injury. As Butchart and Kruger (2001: 219) put it, 'While injuries must... be understood as a global problem, their prevention requires responses that are sensitive to... local-level variations.' They show clearly from their own research how violence and injury in a Johannesburg township were related to overcrowding, traffic patterns, and quality of housing (informal versus formal housing).

For both intentional and unintentional injury, human and interpersonal factors are important precursors and causes. It is reasonably easy to see that interpersonal violence has personal causes and consequences, but it is probably equally important to see that accidents are often not things that 'just happen' – they are affected by human relationships and behaviour. Consider, for example, how commonly alcohol can lead to road accidents, or how sleep deprivation as a result of depression can lead to inattention at work and industrial injuries.

In Chapter 5 we considered in some detail issues arising directly from trauma and violence, and we do not need to go over these again here. What is important for us in social service work to recognize, though, is that issues of injury, accidental and non-accidental, are woven in with a host of other social factors, and have consequences far beyond immediate individual trauma effects. Injury to one member of a family can have devastating effects on the whole family for years to come in terms of economic functioning, interpersonal relationships, education, and even whether the next generation decides to have children or not.

Refugees, migration, and urbanization

The United Nations High Commissioner for Refugees (UNHCR) estimates that as of 1 January 2000, there were 22.3 million people who were what they term 'of concern' to the organization. This includes refugees, asylum seekers, refugees who have returned to their country of origin, internally displaced persons, and others. Internally displaced persons include people 'who have been forced to flee their homes but who have not reached a neighbouring country and therefore, unlike refugees, are not protected by international law or eligible to receive many types of aid' (UNHCR, 2000: 4). The ten countries from which most refugees fled in 1999 were, in order, Afghanistan, Iraq, Burundi, Sierra Leone, Sudan, Somalia, Bosnia-Herzegovina, Angola, Eritrea, and Croatia. According to UNHCR figures, at the end of 2000 there were approximately 594 766 refugees, asylum seekers, returned refugees, and internally displaced persons in the southern African region. It is, however, difficult to keep accurate statistics because of large numbers of undocumented migrants. The UNHCR notes that a particular area of concern in South Africa is the rise of xenophobia: in the years 1994–1999 at least thirty refugees and asylum-seekers were killed in South Africa in attacks against foreigners (UNHCR, 1999).

In addition to 'formal' refugees and internally displaced persons known to an organization like the UNHCR, there are many people who have to leave their homes because of low-level violence. In South Africa, for example, during the 1990s many people were forced out of their homes in KwaZulu-Natal and Gauteng provinces owing to wars between the African National Congress and the Inkatha Freedom Party. Displacements can occur even within cities and settlements where there is a great deal of conflict and violence and, sometimes, gang activity, and people move to safer areas. There are other forms of migration which affect people's lives, including what some have termed 'economic migrancy' – where people move within and between countries in search of better economic prospects. Given levels of poverty worldwide, economic migrancy is often a survival necessity rather than a choice. The entire world is becoming more urbanized, with urbanization patterns especially rapid in low-income countries (Desjarlais *et al.*, 1995), and many cities in these countries not having the infrastructure or resources to accommodate the millions of new urban poor. Cities in areas as far apart as South America, Africa, and Asia, for example, all have a predictable pattern of large shanty towns becoming home to substantial proportions of inhabitants. Migration is not always stable, and people may move back and forth between urban centres and rural homes according to economic and other needs. For example, a woman may choose to move from her rural home to the city during a difficult pregnancy as health care is better in the city. When the baby is a few weeks old, she may return home, only to come back to the city for a protracted period when she sees the baby is not developing well and she feels she needs special facilities to help her care for and educate her child.

Global migration in the postcolonial era is changing the face of the world, with almost every country becoming more heterogeneous culturally and linguistically. In substantial parts of the USA, for example, Spanish is spoken far more widely than English. More than half of the inhabitants of the city of Leicester in Britain are not white and of British ancestry. It has been estimated that in Australia, roughly one fifth of the population is of what Australia terms 'Culturally and Linguistically Diverse' background – people from non-English-speaking countries in Asia, Europe, Africa, and elsewhere. An ironic backdrop to these vast global shifts is that what have come to be known as 'first nations' – minorities such as Inuit in Canada, native Americans in the USA, and Aboriginal Australians – are often forgotten about and overlooked. These groups, which have suffered greatly in the early waves of colonization from Europe, have some commonalities in that they have much poorer health and quality of life status than people of settler origins in their countries. Alcoholism, for example, has been highlighted as a particular problem in first nation communities.

Migration, whether forced or voluntary, recognized by organizations like the UNHCR or less conspicuous, has emotional consequences. All migrants, even if they find a better life in their new context, have to face losses of a familiar home, and they will often lose the support of family and friends. Skills which were recognized in the home context may not be recognized in the new setting – for example, a very skilled rural herdsman with little formal education but excellent abilities in dealing with flocks of animals will find it almost impossible on moving to a city to find any work which needs and recognizes his skills, and a medical specialist highly respected in her own country may find her qualifications unrecognized and herself disregarded as ignorant in her new country as she cannot speak the dominant language of that country. In new contexts, new pressures are brought to bear on migrants, and children of migrants are often caught between the 'old' ways of their parents and the norms of the world they see around them. Every ordinary stage of life is potentially changed, and with populations ageing throughout the world, many people face the prospect of growing old and being buried in an environment very different from where they had hoped to spend their last years. Many people when they die wish to be close to their family and their ancestors, and for many migrants this is not possible.

All of us who work with people will in the course of what we do come into contact with people who have migrated under a range of circumstances; some of us, of course, are migrants ourselves. Often in this work we have to think very carefully and work extra hard to create a safe emotional space which takes account of loss and the ongoing instability of people's lives. It can be very taxing emotionally to try to provide containment and care when those with whom we work have no sense of a stable past or future. We often have to help people who experience hostility and even outright violence simply because they are migrants. In this work, it is sometimes difficult to access the community supports and resources that we would normally expect to be there. For example, in trying to help a schoolchild with educational difficulties, a teacher may find that the child's parents have been killed in another country, that the child is living with relatives who do not speak the language of the school, and that the relatives resent this extra burden on them and have no interest in the child's education. The potential for helpers in a context like this to feel bewildered and disoriented is enormous. Once again, thinking about these issues, and taking time to process them and to share them with colleagues if possible – simple self-help strategies – is very important.

The issues we have discussed in this chapter do not, by any means, cover all those which confront our changing world. It is also increasingly difficult to predict what all the challenges will be. What is certain though, is that broad social and political events will continue to have an emotional impact – an impact that needs to be taken seriously.

Working in a challenging world

The factors which make up our changing world are multiple, complex, and on a scale beyond the control of most people who do counselling. It is, however, both important and useful for our work that we keep the bigger picture in mind. Here are some pointers to how to use these issues to the benefit of clients:

- Politics, economics, racism, prejudice, discrimination, and similar issues affect us all but are often not spoken about. Keep these issues in the back of your mind when working with people – this can help your understanding of them.
- Even though these issues affect all of us, each of us experiences them individually. Listen for the individual experience, the person's own interpretation of history.
- Accept that many people will not wish to discuss broader political and social issues, even if they are affected by them. Keeping something in mind does not mean that we must force those we work with to discuss it.
- Think about your own reactions to these issues. How does your own positioning on them affect how you work with people, your countertransference, your strengths and weaknesses in the work?

- Where appropriate, think about counselling work in a broader context. Are there issues of social justice, access to resources, advocacy and so on which should ideally go hand in hand with your counselling work?
- Think about how best to achieve these broader goals – you will probably have to work together with others who have other skills, or use skills separate from your counselling skills, to make the best progress.
- Accept that your impact as an individual may be limited. Part of the goal of counselling at best is to help others to take action in making their world better. Do not draw clients into your own agenda, but remember that good counselling can help others achieve their aims.
- We do not have to choose between a 'psychological' or 'counselling' understanding of the world and one that looks at political and material issues. Both are important if people's lives – and our own – are to be improved.

Concluding comments

Thinking about personal factors in our work is not a luxury. Even where the work deals with bread and butter issues that seem the result of practical problems alone, there is always an emotional component. Whatever the method of work, and whatever the aims, there is always a human side to the work. If this human side is hard to find or recognize, this does not make it any less important – in fact, the contrary may be true.

This book has not been concerned primarily with specific skills needed for specific jobs. Instead, we have discussed issues that are common to all types of work with people. One of the major challenges the human services face is in the burnout of key personnel. In our experience the space and language to think about the meaning of the work have been crucial in minimizing the problem of burnout. We hope that this book, whatever the context of your work, will help you to think about yourself in relation to whatever work you do. You, and your colleagues, are what you have to offer in dealing with challenges in the lives of the people you want to help.

References and further reading

American Psychiatric Association (APA). (1994). *Diagnostic and Statistical Manual of Mental Disorders* (4th ed.). (*DSM-IV*). Washington: American Psychiatric Association.

Anderson, R. (1996). 'Some thoughts about interviewing the young child'. *Southern African Journal of Child and Adolescent Mental Health*, 8, 68–72.

Beehr, T. (1995). *Psychological Stress in the Workplace*. London: Routledge.

Ben-Tovim, D. (1987). *Development Psychiatry: Mental Health and Primary Health Care in Botswana*. London: Tavistock.

Bor, R., Miller, R., and Goldman, E. (1992). *Theory and Practice of HIV Counselling: A Systemic Approach*. London: Cassell.

Brown, G. W. and Harris, T. (1978). *The Social Origins of Depression*. London: Tavistock.

Budlender, D. (2000). 'Human development'. In J. May (Ed.). *Poverty and Inequality in South Africa: Meeting the Challenge* (pp. 97–139). Cape Town: David Philip; London and New York: Zed Books.

Burden of Disease Unit, Harvard School of Public Health (2000). *The Executive Summary of The Global Burden of Disease and Injury Series*. Downloaded from the Worldwide Web http://www.hsph.harvard.edu/organizations/bdu/summary.html on 20 June 2001.

Butchart, A. and Kruger, J. (2001). 'Public health and community psychology: A case study in community-based injury prevention'. In M. Seedat, N. Duncan, and S. Lazarus (Eds.). *Community Psychology: Theory, Method and Practice – South African and Other Approaches* (pp. 215–241). Cape Town: Oxford University Press.

Casement, P. (1985). *On Learning From the Patient*. London: Tavistock.

Copley, B. and Forryen, B. (1987). *Therapeutic Work with Children and Young People*. London: Robert Royce.

Das, V., Kleinman, A., Ramphele, M., and Reynolds, P. (Eds.). (2000). *Violence and Subjectivity*. Berkeley: University of California Press.

Desjarlais, R., Eisenberg, L., Good, B., and Kleinman, A. (1995). *World Mental Health: Problems and Priorities in Low-income Countries*. New York and Oxford: Oxford University Press.

Di Nicola, V. F. (1986). 'Beyond Babel: family therapy as cultural translation'. In *International Journal of Family Therapy*, 2, 179–191.

Donald, D., Dawes, A., and Louw, J. (Eds.). (2000). *Addressing Childhood Adversity*. Cape Town: David Philip.

Dorrington, R., Bourne, D., Bradshaw, D., Laubscher, R., and Timæus, I. M. (2001). *The Impact of HIV/AIDS on adult Mortality in South Africa*. Technical Report, Burden of Disease Unit, Medical Research Council. Downloaded from the Worldwide Web http://www.mrc.ac.za/bod/index/htm on 17 October 2001.

Doyal, L. (1995). *What Makes Women Sick: Gender and the Political Economy of Health.* London: Macmillan.

Evans, J. and Swartz, L. (2000). 'Training service providers working with traumatised children in South Africa: the navigations of a trainer'. In *Psychodynamic Counselling*, 6, 49–64.

Fisher, S. (1984). *Stress and the Perception of Control.* London: Lawrence Erlbaum.

Fontana, D. (1990). *Managing Stress.* London: BPS Books.

Foster, D., Freeman, M., and Pillay, Y. (Eds.). (1997). *Mental Health Policy Issues for South Africa.* Cape Town: MASA Multimedia.

Friedman, E. H. (1982). 'The myth of the shiksa'. In M. McGoldrick, J. K. Pearce, and J. Giordano (Eds.). *Ethnicity and Family Therapy* (pp. 499–526). New York: Guilford Press.

Gibson, K. and Swartz, L. (2000). 'Politics and emotion: Working with disadvantaged children in South Africa'. In *Psychodynamic Counselling*, 6, pp.133–153.

Gibson, K. (1996).'Working with children in violence: The therapeutic classroom'. In *Psycho-analytic Psychotherapy in South Africa*, 4 (2): 19–31.

Gibson, K., Sandenbergh, R., and Swartz, L. (2001). 'Becoming a community clinical psychologist: Integration of community and clinical practices in psychologists' training'. In *South African Journal of Psychology*, 31, 29–35.

Gilman, S. (1988). *Disease and Representation: Images of Illness from Madness to AIDS.* Ithaca: Cornell University Press.

Good, M., DelVecchio, J., Brodwin, P., Good, B., and Kleinman, A. (Eds.). (1992). *Pain as Human Experience: An Anthropological Perspective.* Berkeley: University of California Press.

Gray, A. (1994). *Introduction to the Therapeutic Frame.* London: Routledge.

Harpham, T. and Blue, I. (Eds.). (1995). *Urbanization and Mental Health in Developing Countries.* Aldershot: Avebury.

Helman, C. (2000). *Culture, Health and Illness* (4th ed.). Oxford: Butterworth-Heineman.

Herman, J. L. (1992). *Trauma and Recovery.* New York: Basic Books.

Jacobs, M. (1997). *Psychodynamic Counselling in Action.* London: Sage.

Jacobs, M. (1998). *The Presenting Past: The Core of Psychodynamic Counselling and Therapy.* Buckingham: Open University Press.

Jamison, K. R. (1995). *An Unquiet Mind.* New York: A. A. Knopf.

Joint United Nations Programme on HIV/AIDS (UNAIDS). (2001). Downloaded from the Worldwide Web http://www.unaids.org on 20 June 2001.

Kareem, J. and Littlewood, R. (Eds.). (1992). *Intercultural Therapy: Themes, Interpretations and Practice.* London: Routledge.

Kets de Vries, M. E. P. (Ed.). (1991). *Organizations on the Couch. Clinical Perspectives on Organizational Behaviour and Change.* San Fransisco: Jossey Bass Publishers.

Kleinman, A. (1988). *Rethinking Psychiatry: From Cultural Category to Personal Experience.* New York: Free Press.

Lanyado, M. and Horne, A. (1999). *The Handbook of Child and Adolescent Psychotherapy: Psychoanalytic Approaches.* London: Routledge.

Levett, A. (1995). 'Stigmatic factors in sexual abuse and the violence of representation'. In *Psychology in Society*, 20, 4–12.

Littlewood, R. and Lipsedge, M. (1997). *Aliens and Alienists: Ethnic Minorities and Psychiatry.* (3rd ed.). London: Routledge.

Malan, D. H. (1979). *Individual Psychotherapy and the Science of Psychodynamics.* Oxford: Butterworth-Heinemann.

May, J., Wollard, I., and Klasen, S. (2000). 'The nature and measurement of poverty and inequality'. In J. May (Ed.). *Poverty and Inequality in South Africa: Meeting the Challenge* (pp. 19–48). Cape Town: David Philip; London and New York: Zed Books.

Menzies, I. E. P. (1960). 'A case in the functioning of social systems as a defence against anxiety: A report on a study of the nursing service of a general hospital'. In *Human Relations*, 13, 95–121.

Menzies Lyth, I. E. P. (1991). 'Psychoanalytic insights for improving organizational health'. In M. F. R. Kets de Vries (Ed.). *Organizations on the Couch. Clinical Perspectives on Organizational Behaviour and Change* (pp. 361–364). San Francisco: Jossey Bass Publishers.

Nicholson, N. (1990). 'The transition cycle: Causes, outcomes, processes and forms'. In S. Fisher and C. Cooper (Eds.). *On the Move: The Psychology of Change and Transition.* Chichester: John Wiley and Sons.

Obholzer, A. and Zagier-Roberts, V. (Eds.). (1994). *The Unconscious at Work.* London: Routledge.

Orbach, S. (2000). *The Impossibility of Sex.* Harmondsworth: Penguin.

Patel, V. (1998). *Culture and Common Mental Disorders in Sub-Saharan Africa.* (Maudsley Monographs 41). Hove, UK: Psychology Press.

Patel, V., Araya, R., Lewis, G., and Swartz, L. (2001). 'Mental health and socio-economic factors'. Background document, World Health Assembly Ministerial Round Tables, World Health Organization.

Ponterotto, J. G., Casas, J. M., Suzuki, L. A., and Alexander, C. M. (Eds.). (1995). *Handbook of Multicultural Counseling* (pp. 237–262). Thousand Oaks, California: Sage.

Raphael, B. and Wilson, J. (Eds.). *Psychological Debriefing: Theory, Practice and Evidence.* Cambridge: Cambridge University Press.

Salzberger-Wittenberg, I. (1970). *Psychoanlytic Insight and Relationships: A Kleinian Approach.* London: Routledge and Kegan Paul.

Salzberger-Wittenberg, I., Henry, G., and Osborne, E. (1990). *The Emotional Experience of Learning and Teaching.* London: Routledge.

Seedat, M., Duncan, N., and Lazarus, S. (Eds.). (2001). *Community Psychology: Theory, Method and Practice. South African and Other Perspectives.* Cape Town: Oxford University Press.

Segal, J. (1985). *Phantasy in Everyday Life.* Harmondsworth: Penguin.

Shilts, R. (1987). *And the Band Played On: Politics, People and the AIDS Epidemic.* New York: St. Martins Press.

Sinason, V. (1992). *Mental Handicap and the Human Condition: New Approaches from the Tavistock*. London: Free Association Books.

Stein, H. (1994). *Listening Deeply: An Approach to Understanding and Consulting in Organizational Culture*. Boulder: Westview Press.

Sterling, C. and Lazarus, R. (1995). *Teaching Lay Counsellors: A Manual for Trainers*. Rondebosch: University of Cape Town Child Guidance Clinic.

Stern, D. (1995). *The Motherhood Constellation: A Unified View of Parent-infant Psychotherapy*. New York: Basic Books.

Stolorow, R. and Atwood, G. (1992). *Contexts of Being: The Intersubjective Foundation of Psychological Life*. Hillsdale, New Jersey: The Analytic Press.

Swartz, L. (1998). *Culture and Mental Health: A Southern African View*. Cape Town: Oxford University Press.

Symington, J. and Symington, N. (1996). *The Clinical Thinking of Wilfred Bion*. London: Routledge.

Trowell, J. and Marion, B. (1995). *The Emotional Needs of Young Children and their Families: Using Psychoanalytic Ideas in the Community*. London: Routledge.

Ullman, R. B. and Brothers, D. (1998). *The Shattered Self*. Hillsdale, NJ: The Analytic Press.

United Nations High Commissioner for Refugees (UNHCR). (1999). *Country profiles: South Africa*. Downloaded from the Worldwide Web http://www.unhcr.ch/world/afr/safrica.htm on 27 June 2001.

United Nations High Commissioner for Refugees (UNHCR). (2000). *Refugees by numbers: 2000 edition*. Downloaded from the Worldwide Web http://www.unhcr.ch/un&ref/numbers/numb2000 on 27 June 2001.

Van der Walt, H. and Swartz, L. (1999). 'Isabel Menzies Lyth revisited: Institutional defences in public health nursing in South Africa during the 1990s'. In *Psychodynamic Counselling*, 5, 483–495.

Winnicott, D. W. (1991). *The Child, the Family, and the Outside World*. Harmondsworth: Penguin.

World Bank. (2001). *World Development Report 2000/2001*. Downloaded from the Worldwide Web http://www.worldbank.org/poverty/wdrpoverty/report/index.htm on 27 June 2001.

World Health Organization. (2001). *Violence and Injury Prevention: The Magnitude of the Injury Problem*. Downloaded from the Worldwide Web http://www.who.int on 27 June 2001.

Yalom, I. (1970). *The Theory and Practice of Group Psychotherapy*. New York: Basic Books.

Index